T0158202

The Parents' and Educators' Manual of Teenage "Rebirth"

How to Prepare Teens for Victorious Transitions into Adolescence and Beyond

Bruce G. Bentley

iUniverse, Inc.
Bloomington

The Parents' and Educators' Manual of Teenage "Rebirth"
How to Prepare Teens for Victorious Transitions
into Adolescence and Beyond

iUniverse books may be ordered through booksellers or by contacting:

iUniverse
1663 Liberty Drive
Bloomington, IN 47403
www.iuniverse.com
1-800-Authors (1-800-288-4677)

ISBN: 978-1-4759-4510-2 (sc)
ISBN: 978-1-4759-4509-6 (hc)
ISBN: 978-1-4759-4511-9 (e)

Printed in the United States of America

iUniverse rev. date: 10/11/2012

For the unknown youth lost in the Waste Land

Contents

Acknowledgments

My keen interest in psychological theory began in the early 1980s with the in-services of psychologist Dr. David Patrick at Mercy Home for Boys & Girls in Chicago, Illinois. In the early 1990s, David had joyously immersed himself in the writing of a book on adolescent treatment when, tragically, a disease took away his young life and his unrealized dream. His spirit as a teacher and mentor lives in this book.

I thank Dr. Mike J. Byrne, EdD, for his friendship, professional support, and critique of the manuscript.

The works of Joseph Campbell and Carl Gustav Jung profoundly influenced me and this book. I am indebted with the utmost admiration and gratitude to them both. Through their books, Campbell and Jung taught me how to live, to love, and to work.

With the deepest gratitude, I thank Barbara Schermer and Dr. Jodine Speckman, DC, for their indispensable consultations over the years. Their sagacious advice was a light guiding me during periods of darkness.

I am grateful to Marie Rose Arong, professor of humanities at the University of the Philippines (Cebu), who provided edit and critique of the manuscript prior to submission. Her friendship and affection for literature brought to life the art and craft of conversation.

I thank editors Michelle Horn and Holly Starley, whose perspicacious critiques and suggestions were indispensable for the final revision of this book. I have a profound appreciation for their art, craft, and gift of developmental editing and content editing, respectively.

Although my parents, Richard J. Bentley and Elizabeth B. Bentley, have been deceased for over twenty years, their influence and spirit live in me and in this book. My father emanated compassion; my mother, a teacher, possessed a will and determination of steel. I thank my siblings—Joan, Rick, Peter, Barbara, Tina, Bill, and Patty—for always being there.

Finally, I thank the people of the Philippines, whose unique, friendly culture provided me with an essential haven for relaxation and freedom to reflect and to write.

Preface

This book is intended as an instructional guide for youth, parents, and educators, as well of anyone who respects individuality and the need for personal growth; self-awareness; and, most importantly, independence. This book does not claim to replace or undermine any psychological diagnosis or treatment. Instead, the material enclosed is intended solely to enlighten readers to adolescent psychology in order to enhance self-knowledge, self-change, and independence. Names of both the school and people in this book are pseudonyms to protect identities unless I was granted permission to use someone's full name.

One of the most difficult and important battles in life that everyone must face abides in the journey through the awesome and precarious world of adolescence. Adolescence marks a special and unique stage in human growth and development. On the one hand, adolescence includes the thrill of novel adventures, such as romance, high school, new friendships, employment, a driver's license, and career considerations. Teens can now produce abstract thoughts about love, music, poetry, philosophy, death, dreams of career, and romance. On the other hand, adolescence initiates periods of anxiety and stress because of the task of breaking the psychologically and emotionally dependent ties to childhood and parents, as well as fears about the future and the challenges of increased responsibilities and independence. In short, adolescence launches the key psychological task of independence and self-identity—a *second birth* into adulthood. Teens who maintain a stance of independence and responsibility usually move successfully toward adulthood. Yet some youths struggle in this passage through adolescence. Based on my practice and research, the failure to master adolescence might detour some teenagers into alcohol and drug usage, gangs, crime, probation, prison, prescribed medications, dropping out of school, running away, truancy, teen pregnancy, anorexia nervosa, Internet addiction, obesity, depression, psychiatric hospitalizations, acts of violence, and suicide (Campbell in Patillo and Manchi 1988, Dowling 1982, Goleman 1996, Peck 2003).

Understanding what they actually experience inwardly with their thoughts and emotions can be an enormous benefit for teens because self-understanding is central to one's unique identity. Likewise, self-understanding tends to decrease emotional conflict within the individual and toward other people. Therefore, the information provided intends to be an ongoing resource for parents and educators to better inform teenagers of the vast psychological and emotional changes that occur during adolescence so teens can be better prepared, experience less anxiety and fear, and adapt successfully toward independence. Concurrently, parents and educators who are better able to understand an adolescent's inner psychological and emotional world are, thereby, better able to grasp and respond to behaviors.

The purpose of this book is twofold. First, the information on adolescent psychology will help parents and educators be better prepared to guide teens through adolescence. Adolescent psychology will be practically applied in real stories about students and me in order to help the reader better understand and apply psychology with their child or student in a useful way. Stories on delicate and tough issues, such as puberty, bed-wetting, bullying, aggressive behavior, consequences and behavioral patterns of physical and sexual abuse, depression, and suicide will teach parents and educators about the underlying causes of problem behaviors.

A link exists between psychology and literature, as studied in the academic field of psychology in literature. Similarly, psychotherapists, like Dr. Albert Ellis, employ bibliotherapy—reading books as an additional means for clients to increase self-understanding and self-change. Thus, the second purpose of *The Parents' and Educators' Manual of Teenage "Rebirth"* is to present stories, as well as guide caregivers to literature, that parents can read or discuss with a child or teen or as an effective tool to increase communication on subjects many consider too anxiety laden or taboo, such as bed-wetting and puberty or bullying and suicide. I've specifically written the stories in this book to establish a bridge between parent and child or teen through frankness and humor and by examining the meaning of "abnormal" behavior. Adolescence does not simply halt at the legal age of eighteen because, like with puberty, everyone matures at a different pace based on psychological, cultural, and life experience. Thus, the young adult, age eighteen to twenty-three (the late stage of adolescence), could find this material useful.

But before I go further, I should tell you who I am and why I wrote this book. I am a school social worker who worked with "problematic" children and youth for over twenty years. During the first ten years, I worked in two residential treatment programs for children and adolescents. Most of the residents had become wards of the state of Illinois due to physical and sexual abuse and neglect. Afterward, I worked for twelve years at Cougarville School (pseudonym), which was populated by students with severe behavior problems. And finally, I just could not take it anymore. My body gave warnings through symptoms of stress—chest pains, chronic fatigue, sleeplessness, and nightmares. Work burnout fried me like an acid freak on a drug binge, but my addiction was to challenging teenagers to become responsible and independent. Often I felt ecstatic doing good work with teens when they produced success and maturity. Yet on days of frustration and havoc, when angry teens cussed and fought with staff, I thought, *Why am I doing this crazy work?* So I decided to take a hiatus from my job and write a book to assist parents, educators, and teens to better understand adolescence.

In my work with adolescents, I made many mistakes. But after much research, experimentation, and trial and error, I learned important measures to assist youth in their battle to master adolescence. Parts 1 and 2 consists of short stories about me and students with whom I worked over the years. I learned much from them because they compelled me to nullify myths about teens and taught me deeper truisms about human psychology. In these stories and in chapter 1, I will describe the stages of adolescent development and psychology, along with providing suggestions for parents and educators to help move teens successfully through each stage. In short, I will explain adolescent psychology in a way that makes it easier to understand. I taught adolescent psychology to students with learning disabilities as young as age twelve, and they often astonished me with their depth of comprehension.

Don't be scared off by the word *psychology*. It simply means "study of the mind." In short, we will attempt to understand how a teenager thinks, feels, and experiences oneself in relationship with others and in the world. Chapters 1, 6, 10, 12, 13, and 14 include sections entitled "Author's Suggestions for Parents and Educators." These sections provide a practical guide on various issues, such as steering youth through the stages of adolescents, dealing with a difficult child or a family suicide, and suicide prevention measures. I hope this information will move the reader toward greater self-knowledge, which retains potential *power*.

Parts 3 and 4 present methods by which the adult and teen might develop a warrior's panoply of armor to face the internal or external psychological battles that they might encounter. These exercises and techniques—which include reading, solitude in a sacred place, recapitulation (in other words, a technique to release one's past psychological and emotional baggage), self-analysis of dreams, and journal writing—provide a means by which individuals can increase self-awareness, independence, ability to release and self-heal emotional wounds, ability to discover unrealized potential, ability to recognize self-sabotaging patterns of behavior, and movement toward greater self-realization and a sense of personal fulfillment. At the end of each chapter, a "Key Points" section will summarize the important parts of the chapter to assist readers as a reference guide.

The stories may appear funny and sad, but they will guide us through the key stages of child and adolescent development. Meanwhile, I will interweave psychological information with stories of some unique children and teenagers who comprise the real life Tom Sawyers, Huck Finns, Ponyboys, and Holden Caulfields. By reading *stories*, we learn from characters how to be the creators of our own stories in life and to discover our unique identities so we can get on the path toward a successful adulthood. I am not going to hold back any punches because the pain of life marks some episodes. But hopefully, we will learn something from these stories and enjoy a few laughs too in this magical journey through the dark, mysterious, and wonderful world of adolescence and beyond with its struggles and joys.

PART ONE

The Death of Childhood and the Birth into Adolescence

This section groups childhood and adolescence together because the two relate to each other. Childhood lays the important foundation for adolescence through healthy emotional bonding with one's parents, social skill development, and academic progress and competency in the three Rs (reading, writing, and arithmetic). Although physical changes begin at puberty, the individual's personality, intellectual capabilities, and sense of selfhood continue to slowly evolve. Puberty marks the separation and loss from birth and childhood into adolescence. So like the ebb and flow of life itself, childhood and adolescence consists of periods of change and separation that can feel like a death—a departure from old terrain and a rebirth into new lands. Children must adapt with each new experience; the childhood stories in part 1 explore this struggle to adapt successfully toward a sense of personal growth, autonomy, and selfhood.

There exist key stages and milestones in human growth and development, such as when the child first must learn and master the task of walking. On the one hand, the child will likely experience an inner drive and zeal to walk like her parents; however, she will also likely experience moments of ambivalence and *fear* about exploring the unknown world of two-legged humanity and separating from the security of the crawling world of infancy. Generally the child will not be successful in her first attempt to walk and might fall down; therefore, she could experience inwardly a sense of frustration and self-doubt about her abilities. Yet through empathy, support, and guidance of parents, along with her own sense of autonomous "will," she rises repeatedly until she successfully masters the task of walking. Throughout childhood and adolescence, there exist similar key stages of human growth and development with similar ambivalences and fears, as well as the exuberance of being victorious in one's growth and progress toward autonomy, individuality, and self-realization. The discussion on adolescent psychology and the childhood and pubescent stories attempt to help parents and educators become more aware and understand the presence of this universal barrier of *fear* that everyone must overcome. However, these chapters also provide information and techniques for parents, educators, children, and teens to help them understand and prevail over this normal obstacle of fear.

ONE

Adolescence: The Rite of Passage

I believe that this chapter provides vital information for parents and educators not only to better understand adolescence per se, but to devise a strategic plan to inform the pubescent youth or teen of the vast changes during adolescence. Change into any unknown situation often evokes anxiety and fear in us, and I believe this stands as a central aspect of adolescence and the core reason some teens struggle through this period. The description of adolescent psychology and the story on puberty below will depict this anxiety and fear. Therefore, we can better prepare pubescent youth and teens for adolescence by providing information—a kind of a road map—about what they can expect and what they need to do on this journey into the unknown terrain of adolescence. In knowledge abides power, and through knowledge youth and adults can become victorious over this universal obstacle of *fear*.

Adolescence marks a time of change in the body, mind, and emotions. I believe this growth period compares to the importance of the first twenty-four months of infancy. Anyone can observe these changes as teens experiment with different attire, attitudes, and opinions. Adolescents simply seek a way to sort out their changing social roles and identities in the world. These changes naturally occur at different times for each person. A general understanding or framework of adolescence proves important. A helpful way to grasp the process of adolescence rests with a basic knowledge of the three stages of adolescence—early, middle, and late. At each stage, teens have a psychological task to accomplish.

Early Adolescence

Puberty initiates the early stage at twelve to fourteen years of age.

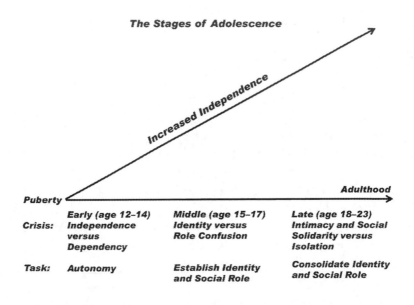

The Stages of Adolescence

	Early (age 12–14)	Middle (age 15–17)	Late (age 18–23)
Crisis:	Independence versus Dependency	Identity versus Role Confusion	Intimacy and Social Solidarity versus Isolation
Task:	Autonomy	Establish Identity and Social Role	Consolidate Identity and Social Role

The Stages of Adolescence

A natural psychological crisis evolves for the youth since separation from childhood and dependency triggers the loss of innocence and the carefree world of girl/boyhood. Movement toward independence comprises the key psychological task. Independence means being self-sufficient at managing one's age-appropriate responsibilities, such as completing homework, maintaining a clean bedroom, taking on a small job like cutting lawns or babysitting, and spending more time with friends. Teens should still adhere to the rules and structure of their parents' household, but parents should be flexible and *let go* and hold youth responsible for the above tasks. Teens will only mature if they face the challenges of life's stresses and the joys of its success, as exemplified in *Harry Potter and the Deathly Hallows*. During Harry Potter's arduous quest to find the Elder Wand, he recalls, "Dumbledore usually let me find out stuff for myself. He let me try my strength, take risks" (Rowling 2007, 433). Similarly, the psychoanalyst Carl Gustav Jung (1991, 56–57) emphasized that the most important function of schools rests not in teaching knowledge but in producing genuine men and women who stand as independent and unique individuals separate from their families. Therefore, if caregivers fail to give youth a degree of autonomy during this early stage, then serious problematic behaviors could develop, particularly during middle adolescence.

Author's Suggestions for Parents and Educators

The following strategies will help caregivers assist youth as they adapt to adolescence and create an environment of autonomy during this early phase:

1. *Throw a celebration that simulates a rite of passage at age thirteen.* A birthday party acknowledges to the youth and family that he has separated from childhood into the milestone of adolescence. This event compares in purpose to rites of passage used in primitive cultures to help youth create a necessary psychological shift from dependent-child thinking and social roles toward an attitude and role of increased responsibility, accountability, and independence (see "Rites of Passage" below). A symbolic gift like a purse for a female and a wallet for a male would be another appropriate gesture. The important part is the verbal acknowledgment and celebration by the parents and family of this developmental milestone.

2. *Teach children about the emotional changes of adolescence.*
   Early adolescence is the crucial time when parents
   and educators have the strategic opportunity to begin
   informing youth about the three stages of adolescence in
   order to help the teen adapt and help ease possible anxieties
   and fears. At this age, teens are less defensive and more
   receptive to this information than in later stages because
   they have not yet experienced the cognitive-emotional
   surge of midadolescence (see "Middle Adolescence" and
   "The Great Barrier" below). Consequently, children in
   this age group generally understand this psychology
   more than older teens because they experience less fear
   of their emotions. Therefore, this information will better
   prepare the youth for midadolescence. I suggest that
   parents review adolescent psychology at each birthday
   or periodically, whenever a *teachable moment* arises.
   Moreover, I suggest providing your child with this
   general information on puberty and early adolescence
   when he or she is eleven years old. Start incorporating
   words like *responsibility, accountability,* and *independence*
   into your conversations as a reminder to the preteen of
   the path she's on.

3. *Provide household chores or informal jobs such as
   babysitting or lawn cutting.* These activities will
   strengthen an individual's sense of responsibility,
   independence, and selfhood. I believe that the simple
   responsibility of maintaining one's bedroom reflects
   on the individual. Maintaining a clean room teaches
   a child self-organization, structure, and order that will
   carry over into other aspects of his life, such as school
   and community involvement. Our bedrooms or homes
   symbolically mirror our identity, attitudes, values,
   beliefs, and so forth.

4. *Discard the possessions of childhood.* At an appropriate time, parents and youth could gather the possessions of childhood, including games, dolls, or toy soldiers, and give these to a younger sibling or relative. This can be another powerful, symbolic gesture of "letting go" of childhood. But if your youngster expresses discomfort with this task, bypass it. The child might not be ready, and you can try another time. These suggestions are simply guides, and parents should use their creativity and to feel free to experiment and discover what works best with their children.

5. *Bestow gifts on special days, such as graduation from elementary school.* During these occasions, rewarding or even spoiling your child is appropriate. But excessive spoiling weakens children and teens; they learn to indulge themselves and depend upon material things, which can breed into a need for instant gratification, a demanding attitude, intolerance to frustration, and a sense of entitlement. Even Jung (1989, 137) reported that most neurotic individuals were spoiled in childhood. Spoiling can make teens psychologically and emotionally *dependent* upon the need for pleasure from external objects when they need to learn that the true reward and power rests inwardly—in self-growth, academic success, independence, and so forth. A maxim to follow stands to simply find a healthy balance.

Rites of Passage

Tribal societies provide young people effective rites of passage that incorporate mythologically based ceremonies. Stories or legends explain the origin of humans or highlight heroic deeds. Initiation rites function to radically transform a youth's psychological thought processes from those of a dependent child into those of a conscious and responsible adult by way of a ceremony involving death and resurrection. Boys generally go through an arduous ordeal of circumcision and a hunt where they are to learn courage. At a girl's first menstruation, a ceremony celebrates her entrance into womanhood. Rituals impel males and females to embrace their masculinity and femininity respectively without cultural or emotional ambivalence. Moreover, initiation rites place the boy and girl in congruence with the demands or expectations of the body— the inner instincts of aggression and sexuality. Thus aggression and sexuality transcend into appropriate social roles for the benefit of the community (Campbell in Patillo and Manchi 1988, 1988a, 45–47).

Modern cultures do not use rites of passage on the comprehensive scale that tribal societies did and do. Nor do they incorporate rituals that provide the necessary "psychology jolt" to radically shift the youth's attitude from childhood dependency into adult responsibility and independence. Therefore, we need to create our own rites, as suggested above at age thirteen and at age eighteen (see "Late Adolescence" below). Today, modern rites of passage are used but limited to particular religious groups or social subcultures. Some well-established niche groups of society with rites of passage include the Catholic sacrament of confirmation, the Jewish Bat Mitzvah, and the upper social class debutante ball. Other rites of passage are more general, such as graduation ceremonies from grammar and high school and proms that serve this purpose as farewell celebrations. Ceremonies and symbols function to make young people conscious of the separation and change that occurs so their natural anxieties have an appropriate acknowledgment and release instead of being denied and possibly being acted out with inappropriate behaviors, such as irritability or alcohol usage.

Yet for the past twenty years, a growing social movement has begun to emphasize the necessity of rites of passage for both males and females in our modern age. Organizations offer weekend or weeklong "initiation" programs that combine activities like group discussions and outdoor adventures (camping, hiking, and cooking) and focus on examining and defining one's womanhood or manhood through self-exploration, self-expression, discussion, challenge initiatives, conflict resolution, and cooperative living. The Mankind Project in the state of Washington, which is exclusively for males from high school age through adulthood, has a mentoring program for males age fourteen to seventeen called "Boys to Men." MKP has local chapters throughout the United States and in seven other countries. (For more information on The Mankind Project, visit the organization's website, located at http://www.mankindproject.org/.) The organization Rite of Passages Journeys, located in Oregon, is for both girls and boys. The organization has two separate activity groups; one is for girls and boys age ten to twelve, and the other is for teens age fifteen to eighteen. These weekend or weeklong excursions in both organizations generally costs around $700, but financial aid and scholarships are available. (For more information on Rite of Passage Journeys, visit the organization's website located at http:// riteofpassagejourneys.org/.) To determine whether such groups exist in your state, simply do an Internet search to find what's available.

In a similar vein, some psychologists and social workers use this "initiation process" in a modified format in group work. The clinicians guide teens through counseling circles, during which teens discuss their key concerns in life, such as school or home. Through games, the teens undertake challenge initiatives that are symbolic of concepts like working together, trusting yourself, and setting goals. Caregivers can contact their local school social worker or psychologist to find if such counseling circles are available in the school or community.

This brief synopsis about rites aims to provide parents and educators a basic understanding so they can creatively incorporate these ideas and methods into their home-based ceremonies and ongoing discussions about adolescent psychology, as suggested above, beginning at age thirteen to better prepare teens for the psychological challenges of adolescence.

The Trap of Dependency

After having worked with adolescents for twenty-two years, I believe the most pressing issue rests upon this crisis of breaking the chains of psychological and emotional dependency from early adolescents (Jung 1991, 56; Campbell in Patillo and Manchi 1988). Psychological clinicians, such as Jung, Erich Fromm, Albert Ellis, and William Glasser, and professor of comparative religions, Joseph Campbell, all generally refer to neurotics as those who have failed to cross the threshold into responsibility and adulthood; consequently, some youth remain imprisoned in the chains of dependent infantilism into their adult years.

My experience and research compel me to believe that adolescents possess an implicit and innate ability to reach their human potentiality. That is, within each of us resides a dormant human potential—our capacity to love and work creatively. The core problem for many teens consists simply of the struggle to break the dependency on family and the culture at large. In the same vein, drug and alcohol *dependency* masks difficult emotions like anxiety and fear and thus serves as a means to avoid responsibilities such as school and employment. Writer Colette Dowling (1982, 110) aptly coined the term *dependency diseases* to describe these behaviors, along with anorexia nervosa. Similarly, smoking and the overuse of psychiatric medications indicate dependencies upon an external substance in order to cope and manage one's emotions, stresses, and frustrations. Psychoanalyst Erich Fromm (1990, 69) maintained, "Mental health is characterized by the ability to love and create, by the emergence from incestuous ties to clan and soil, by a sense of identity based on one's experience of self as the subject and agent of one's powers."

In Fromm's summation, the path toward psychological well-being comes by independence and with the discovery of one's internal capacity to love (in other words, relationships) and create (in other words, work). The enormous problems of teens today, as noted above, mirror as false attempts to establish independence and as *disguised* forms of *dependency*. For example, in gangs, frequently the adolescent becomes an emotionally dependent follower of the group in order to avoid the challenge and responsibility of psychological independence. Novelist Richard Wright (1993a, 91) wrote in his autobiography, *Black Boy*, that, when he joined with his teen friends on the street corner, "We spoke boastfully in bass voices; we used the word 'nigger' to prove the tough fiber of our feelings; we spouted excessive profanity as a sign of our coming manhood; we pretended callousness toward the injunctions of our parents; and we strove to convince one another that our decisions stemmed from ourselves and ourselves alone. Yet we frantically concealed how dependent we were upon one another."

So Wright identified the codependency within his peer group that can obstruct the process of independent thought and action. The research of writer Gustave Le Bon (2002, 2) showed that members of a group lose their individuality and form a collective mind. He named this tendency of crowds to compel individuals to think and feel differently than if they remained by themselves the *law of the mental unity*. Consequently, each member develops, "a sentiment of invincible power which allows him to yield to instincts which, had he been alone, he would perforce have kept under restraint" (6). This sense of power produces a hypnotic effect—like hypnosis—that can trigger a contagion of aggressive behaviors, such as bullying, gang violence, flash mobs, or even horrific war crimes in the military (7–7). Le Bon (9) emphasized, "The crowd is always intellectually inferior to the isolated individual." Yet groups yield positive effects too with benevolent acts of heroism and charity. Awareness of one's individuality and instincts can tactically counter the negative influence of group culture. If group behavior worsens and begins to violate ethical conduct, one should maneuver to *get out* and excuse oneself from the group.

Author's Suggestions for Parents and Educators

Capitalize on teachable moments—incidents of group bullying or crime, gang rape, or flash mobs in the media or community—to open discussion with teens on the important subject of independent thought and action. Le Bon's research contains essential information that parents and educators can paraphrase to adolescents. Knowing that their individual perspective and judgment reigns supreme over that of their peer group can provide teens not only increased self-confidence and independence but, more importantly, a the boost to the inner ego that is necessary for them to take a difficult yet decisive, autonomous stance against peer pressure if need arises.

Puberty and the Loss of Childhood

Before ending this section on early adolescence, I want to revisit the important event of puberty that marks the beginning of early adolescence—yes, the P word that frequently evokes great embarrassment for many of us. The story below is written for the pubescent youth, parent, and educator to assist them to understand and communicate more comfortably upon this often avoided subject. All behavior is adaptive; that is, we modify our behavior to adjust to situations, crises, and key stages in human growth and development such as when pubescent youth acclimate into the novelty of adolescence and experiment with different styles of clothing and language and show interest in music and sexuality. Sometimes behavior can be maladaptive, negative, or antisocial. For example, a youth may attempt to display an independent stance through disrespectful behavior to parents or educators. Usually, the unconscious force in this maladaptive, acting-out behavior abides in the universal experience of anxiety and *fear* of change or separation from the security of a known situation. Therefore, the intent of the story below is to display my adaptive behaviors to puberty in order to help parents better understand adolescent psychology so they may broach this difficult subject and assist their child in adapting positively during this initiation phase.

Visible clues mark the ascendance of puberty, among them spurts in physical development and voice change. Suddenly there is a loss and separation from the innocence of childhood into the unknown world of adolescence that naturally evokes anxiety for many pubescent youth and their parents. When adults interact with children and teens, sometimes a surge of complex emotions and anxieties from our own experiences of childhood and adolescence can arise in us. We need to have a degree of self-awareness so that we can remain objective and not overreact with children or youth.

The practices of solitude (see chapter 12), recapitulation (a technique to release one's emotional baggage from the past; see chapter 13), dream work (chapter 15), and journal writing (chapter 16) are invaluable strategies for parents, educators, and teens to increase self-awareness.

Anxiety is a pervasive force in our lives (see chapter 4), and understanding this force is an important step toward better managing it for ourselves and for children. The story below captures the awkwardness and anxiety that accompanied puberty not just for me but for my mother as well. I had hoped to write a story about the puberty of an anonymous student, but that became impossible. After all, whose trials and tribulations do we understand better than our own? So I am stuck giving an account of my puberty—the last thing in the world that I want to do. But here it goes.

In 1964 at age twelve, I joined the Boy Scouts. Every Wednesday evening, our scout troop swam in an indoor pool at West Pullman Park on the far south side of Chicago. In the huge pool, we splashed, kicked, and paddled in the wonderland of boyhood glee and innocence. I will never forget the first day in the locker room—the place where pubescent girls and boys often experience their initiation into public nudity as they observe the chests, legs, muscles, buttocks, and most of all—the ole crotch! Naturally, we want to observe everyone's physical endowments—sizes of penises, breasts, and so on. Then you can determine whether you are "normal" or whether you look like a clown. On the first day in the locker room, I galloped into the shower. As water doused and cleansed my body, a dozen naked teenage boys suddenly paraded into the shower. My mouth gaped open in astonishment. I observed with horror the frizzy Brillo pads on these teens' crotches. *Whoa, how gross!* I thought. *These dudes look like a bunch of freakin' weirdoes!* I immediately determined that I didn't want anything to do with this teenage puberty stuff—forget about it. I desired to remain in the Neverland of boyhood.

A few months later at home, I hurried to the toilet. I gazed down at my crotch to discover, to my shock and horror, a swarm of obscure, foreign, wormlike invaders. Upon further inspection, these creatures revealed their true nature—the pubes had invaded! Terror struck me. "I am transforming into one of those Brillo pad crotch freaks!" I cried. I immediately declared war on the pubes; I grabbed a pair of scissors and chopped away like a maniac lumberjack. After the clear-cutting, I took a deep breath and sighed relief; I remained in Neverland.

To my dismay, despite my efforts, the pubes returned with a persistent fury. I thought I could outsmart Mother Nature, until, one day, I stared with horror in the mirror at my crotch. Worse than the Brillo pad teen freaks, I had cut myself into a whole new brand of freak—a checkerboard crotch weirdo! My crotch shined with black dots. Depression hit me like a rock. But I am one stubborn character. I did not let the checkerboard crotch stop my dream of remaining in Neverland.

As I recall this next part, I'm filled with the loathing of deep embarrassment. One day I got sick with diarrhea, and while I sat on the toilet, Mom walked in to help me. She immediately spotted the problem down in the ole crotch area, which looked like a war zone. Embarrassment swamped me. A half-dozen Band-Aids and blotches of yellow iodine spattered my crotch. Now don't laugh—at twelve years old, I had never worked as a barber or lumberjack, so miscalculation seemed inevitable. And when I'd discovered the checkerboard, I'd started digging away like a farmer sowing corn in a field.

Mom did not overreact. She stressed that pubic hairs grew naturally at my age and that I should not use scissors. Mom wasn't the type to get into a lengthy discussion about puberty or the birds and the bees. However, she communicated an important message—pubic hairs were normal—and she encouraged me to let go of my boyhood and enter adolescence. Now I could allow puberty to just happen.

Years later, I would wonder what my mother had thought when she discovered my battle-scarred crotch. I bet she felt really bad. Although she towered as a wonderful mother, I'm guessing that, for a few moments, Mom probably felt guilty, as if she'd failed in her motherhood duty. I know she wrestled to cross the thresholds of the "taboo" topic of puberty. And I'm guessing she prayed a whole extra slew of Hail Marys and Our Fathers for my poor crotch.

On that day, I submitted and joined the Brillo pad teen freaks. Yes, I now identified with "them."

As a side note, if I was growing up in today's world and the son of a less understanding mom, I may well have been admitted to the psychiatric hospital and medically labeled an "obsessive compulsive crotch cutter." Doctors would prescribe a drug to control and cure my crotch-cutting addiction, and I would partake in group therapy called the crotch cutter rehabilitation group, where other pubic hair cutters and I would discuss "our problem."

Identifying the Problem

The following analysis demonstrates that "abnormal" behavior is primarily an adaptive response to anxiety and fear of change or separation. Knowing this will help parents and educators respond to these behaviors. Anxiety is part of our human experience, and it affects each of us in varying degrees at different stages in our lives. For me, for example—and in all likelihood for my mother as well— my puberty was a period of high anxiety. Recognizing anxiety and grasping its possible results helps us understand the reason behind behaviors and actions, such as why I cut my pubes.

Change, separation, or possible danger—an unknown—often trigger anxiety. And anxiety can be a clue that we are avoiding something (Freud 1959a, 54). In fact, psychoanalyst Sigmund Freud (56) analyzed that all our anxiety is a byproduct of our first separation from our mothers. So my pubescent anxiety communicated to me that I needed to separate from something; I resisted *change*. I was too young to be aware of the anxiety or to understand or verbalize what it meant, so I acted out the anxiety. Our anxieties usually get expressed somehow if we don't manage our emotions or face what we seem to be avoiding.

Understanding the underlying psychological causes of the overt behavior proves important. So deep inside of me, psychologically, what transpired? First, puberty marks the loss of childhood and the entrance into adolescence: I simply did not want to stop playing with my toy soldiers and so forth. Just like Peter Pan, I sought to linger in the Neverland of childhood forever. Forget that teenage stuff of responsibility, career, and dating—yikes! So I grappled with the *death* of my boyhood and the *birth* into the unknown world of adolescence. Naturally, I experienced some mild depression with the loss of my boyhood because human nature tends to hold on to things familiar and secure—my childhood. Indeed, adolescence initiates a new journey into a dark, mysterious new world with trials, tribulations, and potential boon.

A simple and practical solution to my problem existed; in short, I needed to grieve the loss of my boyhood and move forward in independence. The solution seems easy enough, so why such difficulty? Experience informs me that, whenever we encounter *separations*, such as from our childhood, we come face-to-face with the dark pain of life. Simply put, the separations and losses of life hurt, and sometimes we prefer to avoid the pain by blaming others, remaining immature and dependent, acting out, taking medication, and so forth. So we could describe my crotch cutting as a maladaptive behavior to cope with my anxiety, stress, and fear of change. Remember this; life flows with a series of separations or deaths that bring the next stage or birth in the process of human growth and development.

Author's Suggestions for Parents and Educators

1. *Practice* reflective listening *and* I messages *to help preteens identify and express their inner anxieties and emotions.* At pubescence, some children, like me, may have difficulty identifying inner anxieties and emotions. Parents and educators can help children identify emotions by using a verbal echoing devise called *reflective listening*, where the listener responds in a way that affirms that she accurately understood the sender's communication or emotional state. For example, the listener might say, "You sound happy that you were invited to the party."

The *I message* is another useful communication strategy. I messages convey what the adult senses the child might be experiencing emotionally. For example, a parent may say, "Son, *when* I see you in this quiet mood, *I feel* you might have some mixed feelings about your upcoming birthday *because* of growing up and experiencing all the body changes. Does that make sense to you?" The adult does not tell the child what he feels: "You are sad." An I message contains three elements—(1) what is occurring (the child is quiet), (2) what the adult feels the child might be experiencing (mixed as to upcoming birthday), and (3) why the child might be feeling this way (body changes accompany growing up) (Dinkmeyer et al. 1998, 50–51; Gordon, 2000). In short, the three core elements of an I message sentence are the words *when*, *I feel*, and *because*.

An excellent book, *Parenting Teenagers: Systematic Training for Effective Parenting for Teens* (Dinkmeyer et al. 1998) teaches these basic communication skills. In addition, the book provides a valuable guide for disciplinary methods that employ natural and logical consequences for behavior. Additionally, I recommend *Dibs in Search of Self* by psychologist Virginia M. Axline. Axline presents her therapeutic play sessions with an emotionally disturbed child named Dibs. In this readable and practical book, the reader will experience Axline's skillful clinical expertise and masterful communication (reflective listening) with this noncommunicative and angry child. After a few sessions, Dibs slowly breaks out of his defensive shell and moves toward developing a sense of trust, self-confidence, and emotional independence. As Dibs transforms, his parents change as well. This book is a pragmatic demonstration of the importance of effective communication and a safe and positive environment for a child's emotional needs and growth.

2.   *Find a way to provide kids with thorough, accurate information about sex* before *they hit puberty.* As the school social worker at Cougarville School, I was taxed with the responsibility of sex education. This triggered much anxiety in me. No way did I plan to give a lecture to a group of severe behavior disordered adolescents. Such a situation would likely spark excessive acting-out behaviors. So

I found an excellent DVD sex education program that I recommend. *What Kids Want to Know about Sex and Growing Up* is wonderfully detailed, thorough, and discreet. In the program, two adult sex educators discuss subjects from puberty and menstruation to body anatomy and coitus with students age eleven to fourteen. The program is so thorough that students rarely asked any questions.

Middle Adolescence

Midadolescence (from age fifteen to seventeen) can be smooth sailing for many youth who have developed a healthy degree of independence and competence in the three Rs during early adolescence. My experience with troubled adolescents holds that most of the problem behaviors occur during this stage. I believe that midadolescence is the crux of adolescent growth and development because of the enormous emotional and cognitive changes that occur during this stage.

The psychological task of constructing a stable identity marks midadolescence. A teen needs to think autonomously. She needs to develop a unique way of envisioning the world, realistically assess her strengths and weaknesses, explore and identify her vocational ambitions that would provide a sense of inner fulfillment, reflect upon her inimitable individuality, and learn to authentically and responsibly integrate and express her unique sexuality. Danger lurks since some youth could become ensnared in *dependent* superficial roles or false identities, such as those found in gangs or the drug culture. Midadolescence sparks the big bang of human development—the emergence of a second puberty. This bang is marked by an emotional-cognitive (feeling and thinking) surge and biological changes in the brain structure. These emotions and thoughts flood adolescents like a tidal wave and might feel like an internal psychological war. Now, teens can think abstractly about the dualisms of life, such as love and hate, light and darkness, compassion and anger, death and life. These teens experience deeper emotional intensity with pairs of opposites that compose our human experience such as love and anger. Teens are psychologically challenged to assimilate the prism of intense human emotions, including anxiety, joy, fear, sadness, love, anger, sexuality, emotional pain, insecurity, and the urge for intimacy.

The Surge of Emotions from the Unconscious

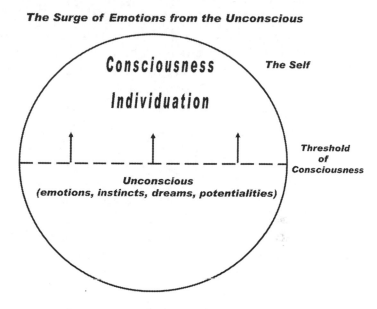

The Surge of Emotions from the Unconscious

Yet with the ecstasy of love comes its opposite—the suffering from separation and loss of a loved one. Just like Romero and Juliet, teens may experience the *birth of love* but also its antithesis—*the pain of life*. Somehow we must find a balance with the ups and downs of life, or else we can get entangled with the attractions of the extremes of darkness or light. For instance, euphoria can entrap humans, whether in the ecstasy of romantic love, the artificial highs of alcohol and drugs, or the idealism of a religious cult. These experiences can ensnare young people, trapping them in the darkness that might turn love into jealous rage or euphoric drug experimentation into addiction and, along with them, depression, paranoia, isolation, or suicide.

Teens must experience and assimilate these powerful emotions in order to move forward in human development toward authentic love, self-awareness, self-control, creative thinking, and what psychologist

Daniel Goleman (1996, xii) coined *emotional intelligence*. If not, emotions may become a fearful threat; thus emerges a tendency to repress and mask these emotions with aggressive behaviors or with drugs and alcohol, which become *cultural substitutes* for authentic independence and self-identity. Yet this surge of emotions carries hidden and disguised potentials. It helps us identify our deep emotions that provide the means for self-knowledge, self-identity, creativity, and intimacy. Emotions serve as a humanizing force and as messengers from our unconscious that communicate via instinct—our deep inner voice.

Author's Suggestions for Parents and Educators

1. *Strongly encourage teenagers to seek employment or volunteer work.* Employment will encourage the independent process because a job teaches one about responsibility and the reality of the world of work; then teens will learn about accountability to a boss, coworkers, and work hours and the necessity of building an employment history. Furthermore, a job teaches financial responsibility and independence. If employment is inaccessible, volunteer work is a good substitute.

2. *Assist the teen to open a bank account.* Teaching teens to be responsible for the money they earn will also encourage autonomy.

3. *Help teenagers acquire a driver's license.* A driver's license is a strong symbol that a teen is moving toward responsibility and adulthood. The subject of drivers' education provides parents with ample teachable moments about the responsibilities of a vehicle with its financial costs, driving and road safety, and general auto maintenance.

4. *Periodically review and paraphrase the general aspects of adolescent psychology from this chapter.* Talk to teens about the importance of responsibility, accountability, and independence; the surge of emotions they are experiencing; the natural obstacles of anxiety and fear that come with change; self-discovery; and work, career, and college goals. Through doing so, you can help young people stay focused on the future. Some teens might find this material threatening and anxiety evoking; it may stir up feelings of self-doubt and trigger the often repressed surge of complicated emotions (see "The Great Barrier" below).

5. *Respond to irresponsible behavior by using this psychological information tactically and labeling the irresponsible behaviors as acts of avoidance, dependency, and fear of independence, as well as possible self-sabotage* (see chapters 14 and 17). Dealing with a resistant, irresponsible adolescent can feel like waging a battle, but the exploration of adolescent psychology will provide you with psychological weaponry and leverage. Used timely, tactfully, and strategically, with the objective of instilling in the teen responsibility and independence, these weapons are extremely powerful. In a sense, you are informing the youth that you know their unconscious secret of inner uncertainty, dependency, and fear of independence and that you will provide empathic support and love along with firmness to guide them forward.

Late Adolescence

For some young adults, adolescence ends at the legal age of eighteen, but others need more time to mature and organize their life goals. The late stage of adolescence encompasses the ages of eighteen to twenty-three, where the psychological task calls for the continued consolidation of one's social role and identity versus a retreat into isolation. Now the young adult should have tentative goals for career such as college, an apprenticeship in a trade like carpentry, the armed forces, or full-time employment and possibly moving out of the home and living independently. Often at this age, romantic dating develops into a more mature intimacy.

Author's Suggestion for Parents and Educators

1. *Throw a celebration that simulates a rite of passage at age eighteen.* Parents can encourage the separation from adolescence with a ceremony similar to the celebration recommended at age thirteen. This can include a basic ceremony or birthday celebration along with a symbolic gift. Compare this event at age eighteen to a debutante ball but for both genders. This important event acknowledges in word and deed the separation from adolescence and the entrance into adulthood with its responsibilities and accountability. Consider this as a guideline and use your imagination to determine what would be the most effective for your son or daughter.
2. *Review the general tenets of adolescent psychology and the task of independence and responsibility.* Engage in a formal discussion with your son or daughter about his or her development. Ask the young adult to present a self-evaluation of his or her progress. The intent of this exercise should be not to judge but to provide a supportive relationship and structure toward personal growth, increased self-awareness and introspection, and independence. It would be an opportune time to discuss the young adult's realistic future plans and goals.

The Great Barrier

The emotional surge of midadolescence bellows a message from the unconscious and refers to what author Joseph Campbell coined, *the*

Call of the Hero. Yes, this is a call from nature or God to duty, to adulthood, and to the journey to discover one's unique identity and potentiality. Yet there exists one universal obstacle that lies at the threshold of our self-identity—*fear.* Psychologist Abraham Maslow (1982, 60) wrote, "Freud's greatest discovery is that the great cause of much psychological illness is the fear of knowledge of oneself—of one's emotions, impulses, memories, capacities, potentialities, of one's destiny." Likewise, Colette Dowling (1982, 57) maintained, "I have come to this conclusion: *the first thing women have to recognize is the degree to which fear rules their lives.*" Author Richard Wright (1993a, 452) wrote of his own fears, "My problem was here, here with me ... I would solve it here alone or not at all. Yet, I did not want to face it; it frightened me ... I returned to my room and sat again, determined to look squarely at my life."

So our external fears consist of an acknowledgment of the source of our fears—fear of self-knowledge. Therefore, as we explore the unknown dimensions of the inner self, fear will diminish. Jung (1990a, 106) specified, "What is feared is the unconscious and its magical influence." That is, we fear our inner dormant potentialities. Fear simply stands at the entrance of the inner threshold and composes part of the inward, heroic path to self-discovery. Yet past the threshold of fear resides the treasures of the unconscious and our potentiality. Yes, beyond the darkness of our fears lies a boon of light—confidence, emotional mastery, psychological and emotional healing, self-power, and fulfillment of our destiny. Fears do not mean that we are weak; to the contrary, fear provides a clue and affirmation that we stand on the correct inward, heroic path.

The internal, psychological battle of adolescence consists of crossing these unknown thresholds of fear in order to discover one's unique identity and potentiality. One essential force or weapon will aid our success in this battle with fear—learning to listen to our deep inner voice, our gut feelings, also called *instinct.* Campbell emphasized that the new brain—neocortex—subsists as a secondary organ to organize information via reason and logic (Patillo and Manchi 1988). But the old brain, the reptilian brain, reigns as the primary organ—that is, *instinct,* which Campbell (1999, 87) coined the *wisdom of the body*. Researcher and neurologist Dr. Anthony Damasio named these instinctive, guiding gut feelings—triggered by the limbic nervous system—*somatic markers* (Goleman 1996, 58–59). It seems that *instinct* serves as a bridge for our conscious mechanism to obtain guidance from the unconscious, especially in stressful or dangerous situations. Philosopher Friedrich Nietzsche (1990, 114) wrote, "One must follow the instincts, but persuade reason to aid them with good arguments ... that reason and instinct move of themselves towards *one* goal, towards the good, towards 'God.'" In *Harry Potter and the Deathly Hallows*, when Harry Potter encountered the Silver Doe in his search for the Gryffindor Sword, he judged, "Caution murmured it could be a trick, a lure, a trap. But instinct, overwhelming instinct, told him that this was not Dark Magic" (Rowling 2007, 366). Instinct operates like an internal wand that we should learn to use in order to create the magic of self-mastery. Therefore, instinct serves as an inward guide for self-knowledge and in facing the challenges of life.

Part 3 ("Internal Revolution") and part 4 ("Self-Analysis for an Internal Revolution") present methods to assist the reader to develop an invisible warrior's panoply of armor to go *inward* into these unknown dimensions with courage and confidence and discover her or his unique identity and a strengthened womanhood or manhood.

Key Points

- Early adolescence begins with puberty, around age twelve to fourteen. Children begin to separate from the innocent, carefree world of girl or boyhood. Caregivers can guide early adolescents through the loss of their former world and help them move toward the key psychological task of this new stage—independence. Teaching young people to manage age-appropriate responsibilities will help them become more self-sufficient.

- A celebration or symbolic gift at age thirteen—following the traditional rites of passage used in primitive cultures—acknowledges the early adolescent's separation from childhood and aids the psychological shift from dependent-child thinking and social roles toward attitudes and social roles of increased responsibility, accountability, and independence.
- Early adolescence is a crucial time during which parents and educators can begin informing the youth about the three stages of adolescence in order to help the teen adapt and help ease possible anxieties and fears. At this age, teens are less defensive and more receptive to this information because they have not experienced the cognitive-emotional surge of midadolescence—"the great barrier."
- Adolescents have the innate ability to reach their human potential—that is, to love with strength and to work creatively.
- Problems arise generally because teens are struggling to separate from the natural dependent relationship with family and the culture at large. They might experience anxiety, fear, and even mild depression with the loss of childhood. We naturally desire to hold on to childhood and fear the unknown of adolescence. Anxiety often signals a clue of change, separation or possible danger—an unknown—and denotes an avoidance of something. Adolescents must cross the threshold of fear into adolescent responsibilities, self-discovery, and independence. The challenges of life make us grow and mature. Caregivers can support teens with basic communication skills such as *reflective listening* and *I messages*.
- Life consists of periods of deaths (separations). We are reborn again and again as we move through life's stages; engage in new and different type of relationships; and

complete challenges in schooling, career, and other activities.

- Midadolescence (ages fifteen to seventeen) triggers the big bang of human development. This second puberty consists of an emotional-cognitive (feeling and thinking) surge and biological changes in the brain structures. Teens must integrate the spectrum of these human emotions such as anxiety, fear, and love because emotions are a humanizing force as well as unconscious messengers that communicate via instinct—our deep inner voice.

- Employment will enhance teens' autonomy and responsibility at midadolescence.

- Parents should occasionally remind their teen of the psychological changes, tasks, and challenges of midadolescence. This knowledge of psychology comprises a huge leverage for caregivers to challenge a resistant teen and, by providing straightforward information along with support and love, to keep the teen moving toward independence.

- Late adolescence ends between age eighteen and twenty-three. The young adult should continue the process of independence by pursuits like college or a full-time job. A birthday party at age eighteen as a rite of passage into adulthood would assist the young adult in this transition.

- Fear of the self creates most psychological problems, but if we learn to listen to our inner voice of instinct, it will aid us to overcome fear and thereby increase emotional intelligence and independence.

- The psychoanalytic school focuses on unconscious motives and forces within the mind such as the sexual and aggressive drives and childhood experiences. Dr. Freud viewed sex as the *tour de force* in psychology. In contrast, Dr. Adler conceived the aggressive drive as the force of dominance in the psyche where the individual often seeks power over others in order to compensate for his or her inferiorities. Dr. Jung construed the psyche as *energy* that expresses itself via sexuality and power in the process of individuation (Campbell 2004, 64).

- Some psychoanalysts and their associated schools of psychology include Dr. Fromm (psychoanalysis and social psychology), Dr. Glasser (reality therapy), Dr. Ellis (cognitive psychology/rational-emotive therapy), and Dr. Maslow (of the humanistic school that focus on self-understanding, creativity, being goal-directed, and the development of human potential).

- Dr. Erikson (psychosocial theory) significantly influenced the three stages of adolescence. Erikson, an ego psychology theorist, emphasized strengthening ego functions rather than to probing unconscious motives and drives. Ego functions include: frustration tolerance, reality testing (i.e., what is real is real), perception, delay of gratification, reasoning/logic, healthy defense mechanisms, judgment, and concentration.

Two

King of the Fakers

Children need love and attention, and in this era of two working parents time is sparse. But what's important is maintaining quality time. The story below is written for parents and children as a tool to further understanding "abnormal" behavior as a response to fear. Moreover, it explores the underlying goals of acting out, or in other words, maladaptive behaviors. While these goals may include attention, power, or revenge, the behaviors are likely masking a sense of inadequacy or helplessness and are often veiled attempts at self-sabotage. Parents and educators must be aware of a child's situation and stage of development and determine whether the child may be experiencing anxieties and fears about changes in circumstances, relationships, or key stages in growth and development.

For children, this story provides various ways of seeking attention from their parents creatively and positively. For parents, it offers creative methods of initiating further involvement with their children in this time-strapped modern age. In addition, it examines a situation some parents and educators have likely experienced—children apparently faking a sickness or tending to play the role of a hypochondriac—offering a view of these behaviors as an adaptive response to fear.

Bruce G. Bentley

Drama: Act One

I don't remember acting out these bizarre theatrics at age three or four, but my mother sometimes gossiped about my faking acts, and it embarrassed me. Sometimes Mom would suddenly find me sprawled on the floor unconscious and shaking with epileptic seizures. Mom would immediately pick me up and pour cold water over my face until I became conscious. It terrified her, and she rushed me to the doctor because she thought I had caught some novel disease. Fortunately the savvy doctor immediately caught on to my con game. He diagnosed me as a faker, explaining that I'd passed out by holding my breath. He advised Mom to just ignore me next time, and I would be cured. She followed his advice, and sure enough, I got up and returned to my business—cured.

Behavior should be examined symbolically, just like the symbols in a story or dream. Most behavior serves a purpose or goal. I sought Mom's attention, love, and physical contact. Mom had given birth to eight kids in ten years, and I arrived as number four—squashed in the middle. I am not complaining, but I felt like a piece of Swiss cheese in the middle of a club sandwich—I'm talking Swiss cheese, not cheddar or American, because of the big holes inside. When you grow up in a big family and your parents only earn enough money to live and to eat week-by-week, it's pure Darwinian survival of the fittest. Intense competition ensues for the extra pork chops, Oreo cookies, and Frosted Flakes. In our house, when shopping finished on Saturday, these goodies became extinct by Sunday at 10:00 a.m.

So this wise doctor spoiled my scam to get Mom's attention. Therefore, I felt compelled to rehabilitate and go on the "legit" and find a more socially acceptable way not to feel like a piece of Swiss cheese. The logical tactic entailed participation in one of Mom's numerous household duties, so I decided to go grocery shopping with her. I remember being in the A&P grocery store on 86th Street and Stony Island Avenue on the south side of Chicago. I sat in the shopping cart in front of the automatic coffee grinder, humming away with the aroma of Eight O'Clock coffee in the air while I savored every moment with Mom. Of course, I still pulled a minor con and asked mom for a Mars chocolate bar. Although Mom really could not afford the extra perk, she always acquiesced.

Then I sought a way to get Dad's attention too. When Pops came home from work at 5:30 p.m., my parents always enjoyed a cocktail and discussed their days in the living room. Like most parents, Dad and Mom each sat in his or her favorite chair. Dad, a salesman, would wear his white dress shirt, tie, brown slacks, and black wing tip shoes. He always sat with one leg crossed over the other. I relished sitting on his raised foot as if on a seesaw, and dad would swing his leg while I giggled with glee. I conned a luscious treat from him, too, because I always asked for a sip of Dad's beer, and that sip tasted better than any beer I have drank in my entire life. The beer tasted bitter, fuzzy, and sometimes spurted up my nose—but wow, what a delight!

Now I realize that sitting on my dad's foot and embracing his leg marked an important moment in my growth and development. The embrace helped me form an attachment to my father; I absorbed and internalized his love, masculinity, and strength. Indeed, it felt like a sacred moment or a new "birth" because I established my *identification* with him as a male and as my father. Moreover, the act firmly launched in my mind a dream for the future in adolescence— to seek a distinct manhood of strength.

What I did next with Dad I relished as the best. At age four, I experienced fear of sleeping at night, so like most kids, I scurried to the security of my parents' bedroom. Dad devised a brilliant strategy for me to remain in my own bed. Dad dressed in a white T-shirt and boxer shorts while I wore blue and white animal pajamas. Dad and I kneeled next to each other facing the bed with our hands clamped together. Yeah, Dad taught me to pray. Praying with my dad shines as one of the most special moments in my life. He taught me the Our Father and Hail Mary. We prayed for my siblings and mom. I have visited the Notre Dame Cathedral in Paris, St. Paul's Church in London, St. Peter's in Rome, temples and mosques in Jerusalem, Hindu temples in India, and Buddhist temples in Thailand, but this moment with Dad generated more meaning and sanctity than all these holy places combined.

Indeed, Dad validated the invisible spiritual world for me, and now I achieved a sense of *identification* with the invisible Spirit/God. I sensed that, somehow, I was implicitly linked to the invisible realm, even though it was webbed in mystery, and retained access to its supporting powers. Furthermore, this encounter initiated my belief that crossing the invisible threshold into the unknown was a means of restoring my equilibrium. So whenever I experienced fear of the unknown, whether in falling asleep or waking up from a nightmarish dream, I learned that somehow the presence of *fear* corresponded to the "crossroad" into the mysterious spiritual domain. Indeed, an implicit linkage exists, and I possess the means to obtain access (prayer and meditation) past the visible plane and threshold into the mysterious and invisible. Moreover, whenever I experience internal discord and imbalance such as anxiety or fear, I can access the spiritual realm in order to regain balance. As I look back upon this sacred moment, it strikes me that a "birth" occurred. Jesus said, "The kingdom of God lies within you" (Luke 17:21, NKJV). Likewise, Marcus Aurelius, in *The Meditations*, emphasized that divinity, which we must seek and cultivate, dwells within us. I remember that, at the moment I prayed with Dad, a dream was born within me—to seek the invisible spiritual realm and the seemingly ineffable.

Getting Love, Attention, and Identification

A few years later, I learned another scam but again on the "legit." Mom always worked in the kitchen cooking, preparing food, or washing dishes. So I tactically finagled time with Mom and helped her with the dishes or set up the dining room table for dinner. My siblings probably thought I'd cracked to do all the work, but they failed to realize that I had Mom to myself. Now I realize that during this meaningful time, I internalized Mom's feminine characteristics and strengths of cooperation and compassion. Moreover, participating in these "feminine" activities helped me develop a balanced masculinity.

If I had overidentified with Mom, I might have become a softy or effeminate. On the other hand, if I had overidentified with Dad, participating in solely "male" activities, I might have developed a tendency to be a harsh, rigid, macho weirdo.

Humans actively seek adaptation and need to experience love. Love provides emotional food for growth, development, and happiness. The human drive to love evokes the power of life itself. We need love more than we need food, drink, or sleep. Either we get love on the "legit," or we turn scam artists like me. If we don't get love, we substitute with food, booze, dope, negative acting out, workaholic routines, endless dramas, and unhealthy or dependent romantic relationships. The con game makes for an easy way in the short term, but ultimately, it fails in the long run of life.

Drama: Act Two

In first grade, I fell back into the faking illness racket again, but I was unconscious of it, and at the time, I actually believed my own "con act." On an autumn morning as I arose from bed, I banged my right leg on the metal bedspring, and immediately my leg felt paralyzed. Initially, I thought I'd gotten a charley horse, but I took this opportunity to attempt to avoid school. I bet that I acquired my brilliant con idea from TV—where kids learn stuff both good and bad. In 1958, the dreaded disease that evoked terror was polio, which caused permanent paralysis.

I had difficulty walking, so instead of going to school I lay on the couch and watched TV for two days. I did not mean to, but I am sure that I scared the heck out of my poor parents. On the third day, before I knew it, my parents had admitted me to Mercy Hospital. Surprisingly, I did not experience any separation anxiety from my parents or family. The hospital enthralled and entertained me as if I had gone to an amusement park. On the first day, I encountered a young patient my age named Jimmy, and we played games, watched TV, and become good buddies. Also, I got tons of attention from a half-dozen female nurses, and I devoured their attention.

Mom visited me every day, and I cherished these moments. Years later, I would learn that Mom rode on the public bus over ten miles through tough neighborhoods to visit me. Doing so stressed her out because she still had seven other kids and home duties to boot. But at age six, I was unconsciously acting out something. I would later feel very guilty for subjecting my mom to this grueling ordeal. But I learned and *identified* with something important from my parents that their marriage embodied—love and sacrifice.

One day as I reclined on my bed, a male doctor scurried into the room and informed me that I had acquired a pass to go out of the hospital. Then from across the room, this dazzling blonde who had to be in her twenties strolled in, and the doc told me she would be my escort. Wow, I couldn't believe it! My escort, Ms. Kelly Pierce, stood five foot three, gowned in a brown dress, white blouse, and blue eyes. Kelly explained that we would spend the day together playing games.

After we played games in her office, she arranged lunch at Pippins Restaurant on Rush Street, which remains open as of this writing. I still remember the place—the ornate flowered figures carved into the brown, wood-trimmed ceiling; the pictures of Chicago landmarks like the Water Tower hanging on the wall; and the businesspeople sitting in dark brown, wooden chairs eating from white plates on the square, wooden tables. Kelly became the woman of my dreams. She commanded a unique *balance* of feminine beauty and intelligence along with strength, confidence, independence, and compassion. So on this day a dream that was an important preparation for adolescence was born—I desired a romance with an "ideal woman."

A few days after my day with Kelly, I suddenly realized that I had abused my hospital stay—the party was ending. On a dreary afternoon, a dozen doctors in white outfits surrounded my bed. Immediately, the carnival aura melted away into an odious atmosphere of impending doom. The doctors whispered in medical lingo and flashed me the evil eye as if I'd contracted a disease other than polio. Terror engulfed me. Now I thought that I had really become infected with some terminal disease and death lurked near.

Years later, I would realize that possibly, after conducting numerous medical examinations, the doctors had discovered I was a phony and diagnosed me as a faker. However, the doctors found themselves in a dilemma because they had to find a way to discharge me from my newfound paradise. The doctors likely feared that, if I caught wind I was to be discharged, I would pull off some spectacular faking act that would ensure my stay. Moreover, I think they resented me because I had built up quite a financial tab as a freeloader; I did not have polio, and I had wasted their valuable time that they should have used on other patients.

In hindsight, I would understand the doctors' tactical maneuver. The doctors imposed lethal, psychological warfare on me. In my book, they played dirty pool. They devised a cabal and set the perfect trap—their counter con or double-cross—the blonde. Kelly was a psychologist, and the games allowed her to get into my head and compose a psychological profile. I think those tests revealed that I was a prodigy con artist, who had a dash of melancholy. A few days after the doctors had entered my room, spoke in their medical jargon, and terrified me, my parents came. The doctors must have disclosed the medical exams and Kelly's diagnosis to my parents. I was elated by my parents' arrival, and so I immediately packed my bags and prepared to skedaddle back home. And on that day, I retired from the faking business permanently.

Of course, the doctors never discovered any evidence of polio. They did, however, diagnose a measly heart murmur. But the real problem hidden in my unconscious was that I did not like school because an older male bully harassed me daily. Maybe the heart murmur actually manifested as a physical symptom of feeling like a slice of Swiss cheese.

Lessons Learned from a Faker

Parents can learn important lessons from my faking act. First, my overt behavior (leg pain) was genuine, but the cause of the problem was psychological. Jung (1989, 158–61) emphasized that research clearly shows how the unconscious can influence body functions.

Often the unconscious and fear work in tandem since it is the neurotic fears of childhood that unconsciously resurface when we wish to avoid psychological, emotional, sexual, and independent development. Jung discussed how a female patient's childhood fear of horses (the origin of neurosis) had sparked a fainting spell, which subsequently led her to be attended to by a married man, whom she unconsciously desired. Jung (1989, 162) wrote, "We know from hundreds of experiences that the hysterical pains are staged in order to reap certain advantages from the environment ... these pains are entirely real." Similarly, Freud labeled psychological conditions such as mind *hysteria*, and he referred to these hysteric psychosomatic symptoms (e.g., paralysis, epileptic convulsions, phobias, anorexia, and the like) a method of defense and an unconscious act of *conversion* (Freud and Breuer 1966, 38, 123). In other words, one converts his or her psychological pain into physical pain. Interestingly, I unconsciously chose leg pain because, symbolically, it meant that I did not want to walk home from school anymore. Incidentally, Freud (38) emphasized that "external events determine the pathology of hysteria to an extent far greater than is known and recognized."

I sense now that my adaptive behavior clearly fits the diagnosis of hysteria, and I am not alone. This condition still exists: In an opinion article entitled "Hysteria and Teenage Girls," writer Caitlin Flanagan discovered that, in October 2011, near Buffalo, New York, a female high school cheerleader had caught Tourette's syndrome, consequently creating a mass contagion of hysteria with a final tally of fourteen females and one male displaying symptoms such as facial tics, stuttering, uncontrollable movement, and verbal outbursts (*New York Times*, January 29, 2012). Flanagan discovered similar cases in North Carolina in 2002, Tanzania in 1962, England in 1965, and the West Bank in 1983. In the New York case, after professionals ruled out other possible causes, such as vaccination reactions and environmental contaminates, the final diagnosis was hysteria. Freud and physician Josef Breuer identified and studied hysteria, publishing their results in 1895 in their classic book, *Studies on Hysteria*.

My behavior and psychosomatic symptoms relate directly to medical research by John Sarno, MD, who published evidence that the mind and body communicate through the autonomic central nervous system. In *The Mindbody Prescription*, he explained that blood flow becomes restricted at the particular location of the physical aliment, which actually creates the physical illness (back or leg pain for example). Sarno maintained that the cause of some particular illnesses lies in the patient's unconscious *anger*, and they would prefer a physical aliment rather than experiencing their anger and emotional pain. In a similar vein, research in *Molecules of Emotion* by neuroscientist Candace Pert, empirically suggests the brain sends messages via neurotransmitters. The brain sends these informational molecules, such as neuropeptides and ligands, not only to the emotional brain but throughout the body—just as the endocrine system (glands that secrete hormones) does—and thus these neurotransmitters compose the mind-body's *biochemicals of emotion*.

Pert stressed that the mind abides throughout the brain and body. Therefore, she emphasized, this research validates Freud's (and Jung's) theories that the body manifests symptoms of the unconscious. More importantly, Pert (2003, 141) exclaimed, "The body is the unconscious mind! Repressed traumas caused by overwhelming emotion can be stored in a body part, thereafter affecting our ability to feel that part or even move it. The new work suggests there are almost infinite pathways for the conscious mind to access—and modify—the unconscious mind and the body."

This modern research by neuroscientists like Pert clearly displays the importance of the mind-body network, not just with that manifestation of visible symptoms but more importantly with the crucial linkage for emotional self-healing, which is a central subtext in this book.

So Sarno provides evidence that *anger* is the central psychological and emotional issue; indeed, I was angry about this bully and, years later, reexperienced that anger when I wrote about this event in my journal in 2000 (see chapter 16). Being conscious of the possible motivations for behaviors and, at the same time, not over-reading them and assuming a problem exists when one may not exist is important. Any caretaker of children would do well to become consciously aware of the nuances of behavior and realize that, usually, behavior has a purpose or goal. Among these are attention, power, revenge, a display of inadequacy, or self-sabotage (Dinkmeyer et al. 1998, 12–15). The internal guide of our instinctive gut feelings can provide us with clues to what is going on—that is, what does the child's behavior evoke in us? Is it anger, worry, fear, or irritation? I displayed a sense of inadequacy and sought to escape a situation in which I felt helpless, so I sparked worry and fear in my parents.

In the '80s, I worked at Mercy Home for Boys & Girls in Chicago, Illinois, where Dr. David Patrick instructed staff to read *The Parent's Handbook: Systematic Training for Effective Parenting* (Dinkmeyer, McKay, and Dinkmeyer 2007). The book provided for me a psychological foundation to begin observing, perceiving, and understanding behavior of youth. This simple method began to reveal the underworld of the unconscious to me. I developed the ability to perceive unconscious motives behind behavior and, thereby, to link apparently irrational unconscious behavior with rational language, which further inspired my interest in psychology. I highly recommend this book as an essential handbook for parents and educators.

Key Points

- "Abnormal" behaviors are typically responses to fear. Behavior should be examined symbolically, just like the symbols in a story or dream. Caretakers should become more consciously aware of the nuances of behavior, understanding that behavior usually serves a purpose or goal. Children may be seeking attention, power, or revenge through displays that conceal feelings of inadequacy and desire for self-sabotage.
- Children need love, attention, and time from their parents. Participation in daily household activities provides a means to spend time with one's parents. These activities help us in important preadolescent developmental tasks, such as identification with our

parents, which provides a masculine-feminine balance respectively for each gender.

- Sometimes we create dramas and illusions such as feigned illnesses, temper tantrums, or arguments. Despite our busy work and family lives, we need to observe and understand the behavior of children, looking for clues that they may have unmet needs, anxieties, or fears.

- Psychological research shows that the mind can physically affect the body with symptoms like paralysis, epileptic convulsions, or phobias for some psychological gain, such as the avoidance of independence. Neurological research suggests that the brain sends messages via neurotransmitters called neuropeptides—the biochemicals of emotion—throughout our bodies. Therefore, we can increase our self-awareness and psychological and physical health if we view the body as the "unconscious," which is consistently sending us "messages" through our emotions (gut feelings, anxieties, and fears) and sometimes through physical symptoms, such as quasi paralysis or muscle pain. Furthermore, Jung and Freud believed that humans have an instinct for self-healing (see chapter 5), and Dr. Pert's research supports the notion of this extraordinary human potential to self-heal (see chapters 13 and 17). The mind-body presents us with this extraordinary communication network that ultimately provides messages and warnings about our psychological growth and the body's yearning for balance and healing.

THREE

A Bed Wetter's Saga

This chapter reveals a segment of childhood that some people would rather extinguish from their memories because it might spark emotions of shame and self-doubt. It addresses the common ordeal of a bed wetter, with the emotional wounds and memories of teasing, vicious name-calling, and bullying that comes with that experience and can leave a permanent emotional scar. My purpose is not to stir up repressed memories best forgotten. On the contrary, if we embrace, examine, and understand these painful experiences, we can bring a healing light of self-growth and wisdom into in our lives. Moreover, I hope that this story might show a present child bed wetter that he or she is not alone in this ordeal and that this period of embarrassment and shame can be transformed into greater self-understanding, self-confidence, and healing. Furthermore, this story and its analysis aims to aid parents and educators by demonstrating that we can view behaviors like bed-wetting as adaptive behaviors that again deal with the universal obstacle of *fear* of an unknown or insecure situation or stage of development.

But before I explain further, I think a whole slew of you—male and female alike—have trekked with me on this one. I might have been the only crotch cutter on Earth, but I think a lot of you teens waded with me on this one. You teen males know what I am talking about. Don't deny it. I can see you now with a look of denial on your face, your eyes shifting back and forth, your lips puckered, and your index finger pointing at your chest. Shaking your head, you say, "Who me? Are you talking to me? That wasn't me; it was my weirdo little brother." Okay, sure. Don't pass the buck on to your little brother. And I know you teen females are likely whispering with coy innocence, "Oh, not me. Girls don't wet the bed." Okay, maybe a far greater percentage of males wet the bed, but I doubt this issue is 100 percent male. So let's courageously admit that many of us have wallowed in a saturated bed of urine at one point in our childhood and stand together in this common human experience.

After I joined the Brillo pad teen freaks, I quickly realized the advantage of being a teen, and letting go of my boyhood became easier. The big advantage was the ability to let go of some aspects of my childhood that I wanted to forget forever. I will never forget the day of my *emancipation* at age seven. Indeed, this day remains one of the best days of my boyhood because, on this day, I escaped the tag of bed wetter—the big secret hidden deep in the souls of innumerable kids.

I vividly remember the day when I reported to Mom, "I didn't wet the bed last night." Mom rarely looked me in the eye when we discussed sensitive issues like bed-wetting, but she immediately glanced downward and gave me a nod and word of approval. Wow! This day reigned supreme over any birthday party, Christmas, or anything. I became emancipated from the chains of shame, self-doubt, and inferiority. Finally, I experienced some control and freedom over my body.

This special day enabled me to become free from the perils of bed-wetting, including the morning wake-up call when I lay saturated in my urine. I recalled lifting my head up and feeling glued to the bed. It felt like Spider-Man had cocooned me in bed—not with wax but with foul-smelling urine that glued my pajamas to my skin. Initially, I always felt dumbfounded and frustrated when I awoke soaked because it seemed like an accident and that I had no conscious choice in the matter. And yet I felt a responsibility for this act, along with shame, guilt, self-reproach, and isolation.

Then after I rose from bed, I had to clean up fast before my two older brothers woke up. We shared a large bedroom, and they would probably tease me endlessly. So I worked quickly to do what most bed wetter's do—hide things. I'd put the wet pajamas and the sheets in the hamper, throw a blanket over the stained mattress, and open the windows or spray air freshener to hide the odor. Like most bed wetter's I lived a temporary life of stealth—harboring the secret—so I always had an embarrassing, lame excuse to give a cousin or friend as to why I could not go on a sleepover. And one object I had to conceal with the utmost diligence because it was a bed wetter's most abominable object of shame and ridicule—the rubber sheet.

Every bed wetter harbors the nightmare that the secret will leak out of the family circle. And if that happens, then you're in deep water because everyone will know and you will wish for death. At school one day, I stood in queue for a bathroom break. This kid, Jimmy Dugan, taunted, "My brother said your brother told him that you wet the bed."

Humiliation and hurt flooded my being, and I wished I could crawl into the ground. My reply echoed the proverbial bed wetter's response: "Sometimes."

A few months later, circumstances unveiled that Jimmy still wet the bed himself! This emerged after my emancipation from bed-wetting, but it provided a good lesson about life. Usually, the bully or teaser is masking and projecting on others his or her own problems of insecurity, pain, inferiority, and self-doubt. Consequently, I approached Jimmy and looked directly into his eyes, and I challenged him about his insult while he was a bed wetter himself. Jimmy sheepishly acknowledged his crude conduct.

But before my emancipation, I had been renowned for my ability to rust out any bed spring made of bronze, iron, steel, or any metal known to humankind. So when my brothers wanted to pull my chain, they called me Rusty. At first, their teasing hurt badly. You bed wetters and former bed wetters know the effect of name-calling. It pierces your heart and soul with humiliation and pain—you just feel like a worthless fool and moron; you feel like the loneliest kid in the world. Most of us experienced cruel nicknames in childhood that we despised, loathed, and wished we could extinguish from our minds. The memory feels like a permanent open wound in the depth of your heart and soul that never heals. The pain can surface at the blink of an eye. These wounds, along with those made by other painful memories, lie in the deep crevices of our inner mind, heart, and soul—the abyss or source where the turmoil and agony of our *pain of life* resides. We fear, loathe, and repress this pain of life with all our strength. Indeed, there lies within us a dormant force of the seemingly impossible *wish* or *dream* for a magical touch of healing—that the internal wounds will be forever purged from our memory and being. So I will never forget the day of my emancipation. I understand now that it was the first time I experienced a serendipitous moment of self-healing and the wonder and ecstasy of feeling whole.

Bed-wetting Lessons

1. Psychologist Frances Wickes (1978, 82–83) emphasized that, although it can have diverse causes, bed-wetting encapsulates an act of *regression*. A child's temporary use of regression or retreat in order to get parental security is natural when the child is faced with a new situation, such as the first visit to a doctor, or when he or she needs extra attention, for example when sick. Clinicians call this temporary retreat "regression in service of the ego." Yet Wickes (79) astutely explains that one of the strongest forces in the negative use of retreat lies in *fear*. So Wickes suggests that the child's fears about the insecurity of parental love or the safety of new situations can spark regressive acts like bed-wetting. I sense this analysis rings true for me, and I will examine two possible causes. First, in large families substantial competition for sufficient attention and love and, hence, insecurity is often commonplace. In fact, the teaser and bed wetter, Jimmy, was also a middle child in a large family. My regressive faking acts as a

device for getting my mother's attention would support this motivation. A second possible cause, albeit more likely, lies with my traumatic experience with the bully at school (see chapters 2 and 16). At age five, I didn't wet the bed in the hospital because I would had been deeply ashamed to watch the nurses change my bedsheets daily; moreover, bed-wetting would have had a profoundly negative effect on my euphoric experience of being in a wonderland during my hospital stay. Furthermore, it was around age four that I would scurry to my parent's room to sleep and when my father taught me to pray. I don't think I was a bed wetter at this time because I would have been too ashamed to get into their bed, and my parents would likely not have allowed me to enter. In all probability, when I returned to school, I experienced a posttraumatic compound effect because now I fell behind academically, and I had to face the continued presence of the bully, which likely evoked anxiety, self-doubt, *fear*, and insecurity.

2. In 2010, I realized that my showdown with Jimmy paralleled a technique that I read in a book. Such a showdown provides a means of action to confront harassment by a bully or when experiencing tension (a barrier) in a relationship. The Yaqui Indian shaman (a medicine man or curer) Don Juan Matus, who viewed all interactions with people as a psychological battlefield, explained that one should face the "opponent openly" and stressed coolness and calmness in the situation. Don Juan (Castaneda 2000, 120) advised, "Always look at the man [or woman] who is involved in a tug of war with you … look up and see his eyes. You'll know then that he is a man, just like you. No matter what he's saying, no matter what he's doing, he's shaking in his boots, just like you. A look like that renders the opponent helpless, if only for an instant;

deliver your blow then." I concur with psychiatrist Dr. M. Scott Peck (2003, 122) who maintained that Carlos Castaneda's books about the teachings of Don Juan compose substantial aspects of the psychotherapeutic process. Soon after the above skirmish, Jimmy and I built a solid friendship that lasts even to this day. Now I realize that, when I challenged Jimmy, it was the first time in my life that I had confronted a bully and stood my ground. I also realize that I have continued to use this tactic against bullies ever since the encounter with Jimmy. Even at Cougarville School, whenever a teen bully harassed a student, I would essentially use the same direct challenging technique, and it always proved effective.

3. I also now realize that my face-off with Jimmy remains an unforgettable memory because it evoked in me a feeling of "aha"; that is, I experienced the thrill and awe of accomplishment and mastery. Psychologist Abraham Maslow (1982, 71) coined the term *peak experiences* to describe these aha moments in life. A peak experience might be a book that "strikes you," an extraordinary sport or artistic performance, intellectual insight, or falling in love. I encountered other peak experiences when Dad taught me to pray, to swim, to ride a bicycle, and to my chagrin even on the day of my "emancipation." These unforgettable activities provided me a sense of self-mastery that triggered further motivation to explore life's wonders. The aha moments in life enhance the growth and development of children and adolescents.

Key Points

*   Bed-wetting is, often, an adaptive behavior or an act of regression in response to a universal obstacle—

fear of an unknown or insecure situation or stage of development.

• Nearly everybody possesses emotional wounds and pain from childhood that remain difficult to face, but if we embrace, examine, and understand painful childhood experiences like bed-wetting, we can bring forth a healing light of self-growth and wisdom into in our lives.

• Teach youth that they can challenge bullies nonviolently by addressing them directly and confidently, maintaining eye contact, and asking them to stop the insulting behavior.

• Providing children with life's unique aha moments (*peak experiences*)—like learning to swim or to read a book—will increase their growth and development.

Part Two

Cougarville School

This section consists primarily of stories of students at Cougarville School, where I worked as a school social worker for twelve years. These vignettes convey events in the lives of children and adolescents with severe behavior and learning problems. And just as I did in the previous stories of my childhood, these children and adolescents learned to face and overcome the universal obstacle of *fear* in their personal growth and stages of development. But for these students who have experienced psychological and emotion traumas—physical abuse, emotional neglect, sexual abuse, the scourge of inferiority, depression, and suicidal ideation, to name a few—the barrier of fear looms greater than did mine or does that of the "average" person. Thus, they needed early intervention; empathy; and secure, disciplined structures that would aid them in self-healing and moving victoriously forward in their personal growth and independence. Each story illustrates common psychological undercurrents encountered during childhood or adolescence, such as emotional dependency, inferiority, illiteracy, inner emotional wounds and past pain of life, acting out with aggression as a means for release and resolution, depression, and suicidal ideation.

This section will show that these abnormal or adaptive behaviors symbolically reflect the past conflicted or traumatized lives of students and their misguided attempts at self-cure. Moreover, it will reveal that the means for self-change, independence, and self-healing is twofold. This transition requires (1) the establishment of a secure environment that instills the capacity to love (to have successful and meaningful relationships) and work (to use one's creative mind and to hold a job) and (2) the solitary, inward heroic path on which one purges emotional wounds of the past.

This section will bring psychology and literature alive, putting a face on the concepts we have talked about in the previous section. At Cougarville School, despite periods of enormous stress, staff experienced a living experimental laboratory through the observations and examination of student behavior. Jung (Jung et al. 1968, 41) wrote that symbols are meaningful whether in a dream or with behavior because both reflect unconscious content. When behaviors are perceived in this light, one can better understand and intervene more easily and effectively. At Cougarville, I worked with female and male teacher assistants who had little or no college education or formal training in psychology, yet they possessed a remarkable skill and acumen in understanding underlying or subconscious behaviors. (In other words, they were able to interpret student moods, behavioral intentions, and potential for aggression.) Many of the staff members possessed a natural *intuitive* and *instinctive* understanding of behavior that most people can acquire through conscious effort and experience. The key component is to link this intuition (gut feeling or instinct) with reason and psychology, thereby better understanding behavior and more effective ways to respond. Despite my skills, I relied on staff feedback, support, and teamwork. Whether in a family, classroom, or school, human beings create a whirlpool of complicated emotions that no one person can sort out. Parental and educational teamwork as a united front proves indispensable.

As we discussed in chapter 2, we can improve our understanding of behavior by simply being aware of the emotions, such as anger or frustration, that the child's behavior evokes in us. Maintaining a conscious framework of adolescent psychology and linking this to "abnormal" behavior can be like seeing another dimension of behavior, which mirrors the underworld of the unconscious. Jung (1991, 51) stressed, "Like the conscious, the unconscious is never at rest, never stagnant. It lives and works in a state of perpetual interaction with the conscious." This awareness provides clues to identify the meaning of behavior and a means for a better response. My hope is that by reading these stories and analyses, parents and educators might increase their awareness of these behaviors and practically apply the principles of psychology in the home or classroom to make parenting, educating, and disciplining more effective and easier.

Four

Cougarville School

The purpose of this chapter is to show parents and educators how the principles of adolescent psychology explained in chapter 1 were practically applied in a school, resulting in a positive culture and a safe, nurturing environment in which students thrived. Despite Cougarville having the most "troublesome," behaviorally disturbed students in the county, visitors usually were surprised to find the premises even quieter than most regular schools. This chapter provides information on the nuts and bolts that created a foundation for a safe, thriving school, where most troubled students felt they fit in cohesively with the student body and culture at Cougarville.

My aim is to increase parents' and educators' awareness that blending ideas or principles of psychology and education (idealism) pragmatically with complex, emotionally disturbed students (realism) results in a program that's in accord with these two often conflicting principles. I hope that parents and educators might find in this chapter practical and productive ideas and methods for establishing a healthy culture that incorporates discipline, creative interventions, and goal-setting and makes parenting and educating easier and more effective.

Cougarville School stands on the banks of the Illinois River just upstream from the haunting grounds of Tom Sawyer and

Huckleberry Finn. The school embodies unique students (K–12) with "behavior problems," students most people would consider outsiders and outcasts.

Why do these students attend Cougarville? You know teens who cursed at and threatened a teacher? Yep, we had them, as well as students who'd been caught bringing alcohol, drugs, or a weapon to school. We had intelligent teens like Holden Caulfield (Salinger 1991) who experienced hospitalization for depression and suicidal ideation, as well as ex-offenders like the youthful Malcolm X. Students who had been abandoned and abused and who sought their vengeance upon the world, like the traumatized dog Buck (London 1990) attended. We had male and female teenagers who had unconsciously experienced the emasculation of their sexuality from the culture at large. To compensate, many females spoke with the voice of Miriam. "Miriam almost fiercely wished she were a man. And yet she hated men at the same time" (Lawrence 1976, 154). But these female and male students hungered for a strong, balanced, and secure womanhood and manhood, as voiced by adolescent Arkady. "Yes, my whole life I've been longing for power, power and self-sufficiency" (Dostoevsky 1981, 86). We had illiterates who echoed another of Miriam's desires. "She hated her position as swine-girl. She wanted to be considered. She wanted to learn, thinking that if she could read … the world would have a different face for her and deepened respect" (Lawrence 1976, 143). We had teens like Gene Forester (Knowles 1975) and Bigger Thomas (Wright 1993b) who denied and feared their emotional pain of life. Consequently, these teens projected their pain into acts of violence and allowed the dark, beast-like part of their human nature to dominate them. We had students who secretly harbored the words of the psychiatric patient Harding in *One Flew over the Cuckoo's Nest* (Kesey 1962, 202), "Never before did I realize that mental illness could have the aspect of power, *power*. Think of it: perhaps the more insane a man is, the more powerful he could become."

A slew of hyperactive teens with attention deficit disorder attended, along with kids like Piggy (Golding 1954), who thrived to identify as the victim and tended to anger everyone they encountered.

You know psychopaths like Jack Merridew who bully kids like Piggy to compensate for their inferiority and self-hate? A few "Merridews" were enrolled as well. We had chronic truants like Tom Sawyer (Twain 2004), who experienced regular school as a bore, and teens like Huck Finn (Twain 1981) who couldn't concentrate in school because their parents had become alcoholics or violent abusers and only wanted their kids' money. We had students who, like the puppy in *White Fang* born half dog and half wolf (London 2001), felt enormous confusion and isolation because they didn't fit in any social group.

In order to effectively teach, discipline, control, and care for these students, who were often needy and frequently acted out, the staff needed compassion, innovation, intelligence, effective communication skills, and a sense of humor. Fortunately, most of the staff at Cougarville fulfilled these requirements. For example, Mr. Bosky would actually conduct academic lectures to his high school students—just like in a regular school. Whenever I observed his discourse, I was amazed at his magical touch, his skillful oratory and pedagogy, along with his accomplished command of the classroom. Mr. Francois, an excellent teacher for the seventh and eighth graders, had a practical, effective, and creative philosophical approach—"keep the students busy." Schoolwork was not just for learning; it installed "structure" that maintained a sense of order and control. In addition, Mr. Francois believed that students had to laugh and have fun every day in school in order to motivate them to attend and learn; as a result, attendance at Cougarville was consistently about 95 percent, and truancy was rare. Mr. Francois, like most of the staff, had a command of "hyperbole" to make students laugh and think over their "abnormal" behaviors, such as when staff would identify and relabel acting out behavior as childish "temper tantrums" instead of "psychologically disturbed behaviors." Moreover, the staff would let the students know that, despite their academic or home problems, they generally had more control of their behavior than they might be aware of. The staff's use of hyperbole provided an emotional release of stress for us as well so we could have fun on the job. Many students thought some of the staff members were a bit zany, but they knew we cared about them, and they communicated this through their excellent attendance.

Occasionally, though, the staff experienced acute work stress when a student became a danger to him or herself or to others and had to be physical restrained. During these situations, staff sometimes sustained injuries. The staff injury catalog include bruised ribs, cuts and bruises, split head wounds that required stitches, back strains, and stress to the point of heart failure that required hospitalization. At times, we were punched in the face and chest or kicked in the gonads. We endured countless physical threats, broken eyeglasses, and torn shirts and pants. But the staff always had the attitude that these altercations were just part of the job. Both female and male staff received physical restraint training annually, and we took this instruction seriously because "hands-on" was the last stratagem before calling the police. Therefore, through the staff's compassion, teaching, relationship building, discipline, and if necessary physical restraint, we created two important tenets for a school—the discipline of "tough love" and a healthy culture.

The Power of Healthy Culture

The staff might act daffy sometimes, but we loved these students like own children. Every morning as the students entered the school building, we greeted them with a "good morning" and expressed our love in word and deed. However, we improvised unorthodox and radical methods in order to most effectively manage and teach students with severe behavioral and psychological problems. If students only needed a little soft love, they would have remained in "regular" school. So we had to be creative. The staff didn't proclaim perfection; we made mistakes. And like the students, we experienced bad days and, at times, perhaps imposed discipline too quickly or harshly. But just as parents don't need to be perfect, we didn't either. What was important was that we were good enough caregivers—that is, we needed to be fair, consistent, compassionate, and firm.

Although the most difficult students attended Cougarville, the school remained safe and quiet. The staff enacted firm and fair discipline, and the students actively learned. If a bullying or racial problem arose, staff would deal with the involved individuals and issues immediately and directly by diffusing the conflict and emphasizing that the staff was responsible for a safe school and would not tolerate threats or disrespectful name-calling; meanwhile, staff stressed that students were responsible for focusing on learning and success; this approach restored school and role "boundaries." Of course, occasional behavior problems did arise, particularly with new students who, after a honeymoon period, usually wanted to tests the limits of the program and staff. After the staff faced and challenged a student who was acting out, the student generally became part of the student body and positive culture in the school. About 40 percent of the students eventually returned to their district schools. The students couldn't compete academically with the best because most possessed learning disabilities and came from poverty. These disadvantaged students did well because we *created a healthy culture.*

Just as the womb holds the fetus or a kindergarten class with its toys and games promotes a wonderland for social play and intellectual stimulation, creativity, and imagination, a healthy, *nurturing* culture provides a place where students can flourish. However, in a learning environment designed for older children and adolescents, it is important that the culture allows the students to take on increased responsibility and grow more independent and steers them away from psychological dependency.

Conflict, from gang violence in a community to family problems at home, can put enormous stress on a student's ability to concentrate in the classroom. Parents and educators have limited control over their communities; however, they can influence their homes, classrooms, and schools. Establishing one's home or school as a separate entity from a troubled community can be hard work, but doing so is indispensable. At Cougarville, we worked diligently to maintain a secure and healthy culture. For example, we had a group of rough students who had been labeled gangbangers. One morning, this group strolled off the bus, their behavior boisterous and potentiality aggressive. They were, essentially, bringing their neighborhood's gang values into the school. The moment they walked in the building, I said firmly, "Gentlemen, leave the neighborhood in the neighborhood. You are in school now to learn and to succeed."

They sheepishly quieted down. They understood what I'd implied. Whether in a home or school, boundaries must be established, along with the values of safety and success.

A simple formula by which to establish a positive culture in one's home or school is to instill the "emotional" three Rs from psychiatrist William Glasser's book *Reality Therapy*. Glasser maintained that individuals have the universal need for love and self-worth, but they must pursue these needs responsibly, realistically, and ethically (right versus wrong):

1. We should maintain a firm stance on individual *responsibility* for behavior and the rules or laws of the environment.

2. We should consistently link the responsibility and accountability of the individual to the *reality* of everyday life, such as independence, career, university, marriage, family, and civil society.

3. We should unequivocally uphold the common sense ethical values of *right* versus wrong conduct (Glasser 1990, 5–13).

It stands important to reframe these three Rs—like responsibility— as a means toward human self-power and a strengthened manhood or womanhood. For example, someone who acts with "responsibility" is reliable and independent; being "realistic" means displaying self-awareness; and being ethical means exhibiting virtue, compassion, and wisdom. A strong person does not yield to wrong behavior, and it takes strength to take responsibility and to admit mistakes.

Over time, parents commonly reported improved behavior and, consequently, often did not want their children to return to mainstream school. They feared a return of the previous negative behaviors. The students' experience of the positive culture at Cougarville carried over into the home, which was our intended objective.

So a healthy culture enhances the safety, security, and potentiality for human growth and development. At Cougarville, the staff created a healthy culture so students could thrive, excel socially, and master learning skills. In *Tuesdays with Morrie* (Albom 1997, 35–36), the sagacious Morrie Schwartz, a retired sociology professor and terminally ill patient, spoke to the importance of creating a healthy culture. "The culture we have does not make people feel good about themselves," he said. "We're teaching the wrong things. And you have to be strong enough to say if the culture doesn't work, don't buy it. Create your own. Most people can't do it."

Someone questioned Freud on what a normal person should strive to do well at. Freud counseled, "To love and to work" (Erikson 1968, 136). This axiom was the foundation at Cougarville. Love and work are the centralized basis of many theories of psychology and of the great religions.

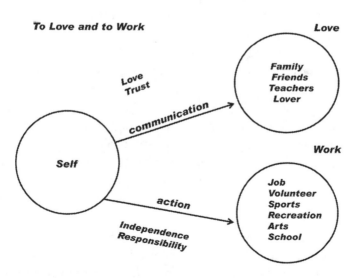

To Love and to Work

Maslow (1982, 30–31) wrote that mastery of love and work builds self-confidence and self-esteem for, "Growth is, *in itself,* a rewarding and exciting process, e.g., the fulfilling of yearnings and ambitions, like that of being a good doctor; the acquisition of admired skills, like playing the violin or being a good carpenter; the steady increase of understanding about people or about the universe, or about oneself … simply the ambition to be a good human being."

Allow me to share a typical playground scene—a scene the staff members would give our lives to defend in the event someone tried to take such moments away from our students. Students—ages six to eighteen, racially mixed, and 85 percent male—play basketball and football, walk, converse, laugh, and joke. The students socialize across the lines of race, gender, and age. For these outsiders, who never fit in at a regular school, Cougarville is *their* school—the place where they thrive and grow socially and academically. In *A Portrait of the Artist as a Young Man*, the adolescent Stephen Dedalus translated St. Thomas Aquinas's definition of beauty as, "*Three things are needed for beauty, wholeness, harmony, and radiance*" (Joyce 1976, 212). Accordingly, the above scene is one of beauty, and watching it is like watching a radiant sunrise or sunset. Culture should resound as a creative force that *beautifies.*

The wholeness and harmony manifested in a safe school that maintains an environment where security, respect, and responsibility allow students to experience aha moments (peak experiences) (Maslow 1982; see chapter 3). They are able to achieve social and educational mastery. And it is usually through these the moments that the radiance of the human spirit shines outwardly. When we observe a child performing on a higher level of excellence—be it in adding numbers, reading, athletics, music, theater, or painting—we often say, "She did that beautifully." This breakthrough of human radiance embodies Aquinas's definition of beauty.

Positive culture creates a protective shield to ward off an insidious unconscious force that emerges in all cultures—*anxiety.* Often students harbor so much anxiety from their lives that they feel compelled to act out with aggression, apathy, depression, and alcohol and drug usage. The ubiquitous force of anxiety penetrates all cultures. As psychoanalyst and anthropologist Géza Róheim (1968, 81–82) wrote that *"defense systems against anxiety are the stuff that culture is made of* and that therefore specific cultures are structurally similar to specific neuroses."

Róheim's profound insight maintained that specific cultures portray a general social character such as depressive, schizophrenic, narcissistic, or passive-aggressive. For example, since the 1970s, social critics like Christopher Lasch, who authored *The Culture of Narcissism: American Life in an Age of Diminishing Expectation*, have maintained that our culture has become increasingly narcissistic—an unrealistic sense of self-grandeur (Lasch 1991, 10). Lasch shows that in the '60s and '70s, narcissistic psychological disorders had become the prevalent diagnosis; he maintained that the changing socioeconomic society (macrocosm) was consequently affecting the family structure and individual psychological development (microcosm). Lasch held that, over the decades, the family has declined in importance because parental authority has been slowly giving way to the bureaucratic and technological society with its enormous external influences on families and children through the mass media, schools, and peer groups (35, 238). In the same vein, according to sociologist David Riesman, who presciently published his book, *The Lonely Crowd: A Study of the Changing American Character* in 1950, these socioeconomic changes led children to develop a new character. Whereas, previously, children were typically autonomous, innovative, and goal-oriented ("inner-directed"), the typical personality of a child has evolved and children are more dependent on others, such as peers or mass media for guidance and self-affirmation ("other-directed") (Riesman et al. 1950, 30, 37–8, 286–87). Meanwhile, Lasch holds that this new character type is primarily a narcissistic personality, who consequently experiences inwardly a dependent need on others to affirm and validate his or her self-worth and as a means of mollifying his or her inner feeling of emptiness and inauthenticity (Lasch 1991, 33–35). As Róheim claimed above, this cultural social character mostly serves as a defense to ward off anxiety. For example, the narcissist claims superiority, but narcissism serves as a defense by which people repress their inferiority and depression. This anxiety tends to be related to the denial and management of anger and aggression.

For instance, I live in the Philippines, where aggressive acts are frowned upon, almost taboo. In this unique, friendly Asian culture, the social norm maintains social harmony and order, and it proves effective. But aggression is still expressed, although passive-aggressively, in behaviors such as ignoring, silence, and swindling. Meanwhile, in the United States, a Western culture of individualism, aggressive behavior arises with more frequency and directness, whether in business transactions, athletics, or gun violence. Yet interestingly, Western culture is considered a *depressive culture* (Storr 1970, 90). Statistical data, such as that found in the 2003 National Comorbidity Study supported by the National Institutes of Health— which found that 16 percent of the population or approximately 35 million Americans deal with severe depression—support the notion that US culture is depressive (see "Depression," http://www. indepression.com/depression-statistics.html; accessed November 10, 2011). Psychologist Daniel Goleman (1996, 276) maintained that international data on the increase of depression in modern societies in the '80s and '90s points to a marshaling in of an Age of Melancholy for the twenty-first century, just as the twentieth century was considered the Age of Anxiety. Moreover, depression is the major precipitating factor that leads an individual into psychiatric treatment (Peck 2003, 58). In *Human Aggression*, Dr. Anthony Storr (1970, 80) analyzed that depression implicitly relates to aggression because individuals "have been unable to come to terms with their own aggressive drive. In such individuals, aggression is either repressed and turned inwards against the self; or else disowned and attributed to others; or else expressed in explosive and childish forms … These individuals have been unable to integrate their aggression in a positive way, and can therefore be regarded as mentally ill or maladjusted."

Róheim claims this cultural social character mostly serves as a defense to ward off anxiety. Therefore, Róheim's and Storr's points of view provide a useful analytical tool to observe and critique a nation's culture or subcultures like schools. We can experience this unconscious anxiety when we observe the news on television as the media broadcasts stories about terrorism, crime, disease, or financial collapse.

At Cougarville, in an uncanny way, we identified as fanatical adherents to Caulfieldian philosophy because Holden held an aversion for phonies. The staff maintained that, beneath the aggressive or insane behavior of students, resided a human being with the potential to love and create. Therefore, our direct, tactical, and tenacious approach presupposed that students embodied a dormant strength and ability to change and be the dream of their potentiality. We enacted the roles of *destroyers* of the old, phony behaviors students learned and imitated from childhood, the media, and in the culture at large. The staff mimicked black holes because we acted as *destroyers*, not of old galaxies, but of dependent, childlike behaviors and thinking. Moreover, the staff mobilized as *creators*, not of new galaxies, but of a new culture, where students learned new behaviors within a culture of safety, security, and vibrancy.

Mr. Francois posted in his classroom a slogan that stated, "We practice assertive discipline here." The staff had an expression about challenging behavior— "Nip it in the bud" from the first day of school and onward. For example, common problem behaviors included refusal to do class work or remain seated at a desk, explosive tempers, poor attention, and hitting students. When staff members challenged these behaviors with consistent discipline along with logical consequences, the students didn't receive any pleasure from acting out; rather, they realized there were limits and consequences. Students needed to experience that acting out would not be fun and would have disciplinary consequences, such as after-school suspension or missing recess time. Consequences must have some leverage upon the youth for it to be effective. Initially, discipline is hard work, but doing so will make the job of discipline easier in the long term, and in the end, staff members helped to create changed human beings.

For parents at home, if children blatantly neglect homework or chores, the natural and logical consequences could initially involve restriction of the child's mobility, possibly limiting them to their bedroom only. If that doesn't work, the next options include the loss of the privileges, including cell phone, computer, and TV access and so forth (see also chapter 6). As the writers Dinkmeyer et al. (1998) pointed out, consequences should be logical to the problem behavior.

Clinicians refer to the window of opportunity immediately after a conflict arises as a *teachable moment*. During this calm after the storm, consequences prove effective, and the child recognizes his or her error. This is a key moment when the adult can review the incident and point out alternative ways to behave. Parents can reassure the child of their love and stress that they will always maintain discipline (in other words, tough love) and uphold their parental responsibility so that the child can become independent and accountable. In short, the adult models to the child how to manage conflict, and out of conflict, there exists an opportunity for emotional maturity, self-understanding, and an enrichment of the relationship, which is the essence of family or school experience. During these teachable moments, teens and parents can both grow in self-understanding. These authentic emotional moments create an inner emotional harmony called *attunement* (Goleman 1996, 59–60) that enables the child to enhance his or her ability to develop emotional intelligence such as self-awareness and empathy.

In fact, psychiatrist David Stern (Goleman 1996, 113–14) emphasized that, during these unique, attuned teachable moments, we can build the ABCs of emotional learning. Parents cannot only help their child learn new emotional responses, they can actually help strengthen the neural circuitry of their child's emotional brain, a process that neuroscientists call *pruning* (256—57). Through conflict and discipline, we can participate as a creative force of change within the child and within ourselves. In short, we must model the soft hand of human love and the hard hand of assertive discipline so the youth can integrate these seemingly contradictory emotions and thoughts within themselves and develop into strong men and women.

Although managing aggression is an arduous and complex task, staff members at Cougarville modeled positive uses of human aggression by creating a safe environment that eliminated fighting and bullying. As psychiatrist Anthony Storr (1970, 49) stressed, "One important function of the aggressive drive is to ensure that the individual members of a species can become sufficiently independent to fend for themselves, and thus, in their time, to become capable of protecting and supporting the young."

Thus, the staff modeled aggression positively, not only to maintain school safety but also so students could experience positive aggression as normal, which would assist them to internalize this powerful force for self-knowledge and self-empowerment and move toward independence. Storr (1970, 50) wrote that if a "child is to feel safe both from external danger and from the threat of his own internal aggressive feelings, he must be convinced that his parents [and teachers] are able to cope both with the world and with himself; and some modern parents are so compliant and so overanxious not to display any aggression at all that they fail to convince their children that they are competent to deal with either."

When parents and educators apply the psychological theories of Freud, Maslow, Storr, and the rest, concurrently practicing strong discipline and tough love and teaching kids the three Rs, *magic* happens. And that magic combines social and educational mastery and a little fun.

Key Points

- Applying the principles of adolescent psychology can alter a household or a school's culture positively; through seizing teachable moments, modeling appropriate outlets of aggression, and using effective discipline, adults create an environment and values that ensure safety, de-escalate anxiety, and promote responsibility and independence and meaningful relationships.

- Parents and educators don't need to be perfect caregivers. Rather, they need to be fair, consistent, compassionate, and firm.
- Create a healthy culture at home or at school by emphasizing that children can get their needs of love and self-worth fulfilled through Dr. Glasser's "emotional" three Rs—by taking *responsibility* for one's life and goals, by taking action toward those goals based on the *realistic* and practical processes of everyday life, and by adhering to ethical, societal values of *right* versus wrong in one's behavior and actions.
- Incorporate Dr. Freud's principle of "to love and to work" by emphasizing two essentials—(1) relationship building and (2) external activities, such as academic learning, athletics, theater, or a job. These two activities will establish a solid foundation for a student's growth in skills that will move him or her toward independence. "To love and to work" summarizes the principles of most psychological theories and the great religions.
- Anthropological and psychological research indicates that all social cultures produce "anxiety"; however, healthy cultures in schools and in one's home can ward off this powerful force and provide a milieu of safety and nurture.
- After a parent imposes a disciplinary measure with his or her child, often a *teachable moment* will surface when parent and child can discuss objectively and genuinely the circumstances of the "conflict" and resolidify their relationship. This authentic emotional interchange is called *attunement*, and it increases the child's capacity for self-awareness and empathy. Neuroscientists have shown that these attuned teachable moments can amplify the neurological structures in the child's emotional brain—referred to as *pruning*.
- Psychological research shows that the aggressive drive's primary purpose is to provide individuals the ability to

independently repel any threat to themselves or their families. Therefore, caregivers must demonstrate and model to children that they can confidently express aggressive feelings and, if necessary, take appropriate action to maintain a safe environment. If aggressive feelings are denied, then aggression can transmute into depression and can get acted out in belligerent behavior toward other people. Western cultures like that of the United States are known as depressive cultures.

- Children and teens need to learn how to integrate their aggression in a positive way, such as asserting their independence. Otherwise, they might become dependent and helpless adults in the future.

FIVE

Rafael: A Journey into the Dark Labyrinthine Underworld of Adolescence

Chapters 5 and 6 tell the stories of two students, Rafael and Charles. My experiences with these students stand out as two of the most aggressively dangerous and anxiety provoking moments of my twenty-two-year career. They capture succinctly the potential volatility of midadolescence as young people struggle with fear, discovering their own identity, and sorting out the powerful surge of emotions—the Great Barrier—they face at this age. The stories demonstrate the danger of aggressively acting out these inner fears and emotional pain (see chapter 1). In addition, they epitomize the crucial linkage between childhood and adolescence and the indispensable importance of early emotional bonding, nurture, and parental love, along with a foundation in the academic three Rs.

Staff members appropriately faced the students' aggression and returned safety and security to the school. Thus, these dangerous situations opened windows of opportunity to understand what lurks beneath the mask of aggression. There lay feelings of inferiority and illiteracy—the students' emotional pain of life. Discovering this allowed for healing and growth for one student. The staff and

I increased our knowledge, grew personally, and took our clinical skills to a higher plane, thereby enhancing the positive culture of the school. In short, challenging difficult youth like Rafael and Charles can be a means of personal and professional growth, and more importantly, we can discover that behind the bravado of aggression lies a fearful, wounded child who yearns for healing.

On a typical calm morning at Cougarville, students had finished breakfast and sat at their desks to work on assignments. As I entered my office, I suddenly heard a shrieking yell from a high school classroom—the strident voice warned of danger. Whenever the staff heard such a noise, we would brace ourselves like firemen jolted by the initial fire alarm. I hoped for a minor incident, like a temper tantrum, that would quickly resolve itself without confrontation.

Staff knowledge of students proved indispensable; therefore, we generally could identify the problem student beforehand. My instinctive suspicion enveloped me with dread because I sensed the yell came from a new student, and we would likely encounter the nebulous and dangerous underworld of adolescent aggression.

I felt a surge of anxiety, fear, and adrenaline, but paradoxically, these ingredients transformed into fuel and armor for my journey into the unpredictable and dangerous world I was about to enter. Anxiety and fear became warning and cautionary forces; adrenaline provided a force for action. Balance proved vital, though. Too much fear could paralyze, and excessive use of adrenaline might injure. Indeed, I needed to be vigilant and harness my emotions and mind in sync for psychological war. If aggression remains unchallenged, then the forces of violence may be unleashed, along with ensuing bedlam. As cosmologist Stephen Hawking (1989, 108) wrote, "Disorder will tend to increase if things are left to themselves."

I immediately exited my office and hurried down the hall. I scanned the hallways for signs of danger—thought in accord with instinct. In this submergence into the dark underworld of aggression, there exists one instinctive maxim—*lean toward the light* (Campbell in Patillo and Manchi 1988). I entered the classroom the cry had come from, my fears and instincts were immediately confirmed. Rafael, a sixteen-year-old gang member recently released from a juvenile detention center, loomed in front of the class. Of average height and weight, Rafael wore a short sleeve T-shirt, baggy pants, and gym shoes. Tattoos signifying gang affiliation, such as crowns and pitch forks, decorated his arms.

Rafael was in a state of rage, and he brandished a brown, metal folding chair, prepared for battle. In that moment, Rafael reigned supreme, for through his aggression, he had what he believed was power and domination. The tension in the classroom felt like a subzero cold. To the far right, the two teachers, Ms. Jones and Ms. Paul, stood rigidly frozen by fear. The students sat at their desks. Most looked down, but they stole furtive glances. Their faces displayed a paradox. Most students smirked, for the thrill of adolescent anarchy may ring true, but actually, the smiles masked fear—the fear of disorder—for if one student or staff wasn't safe, no one was. The students wondered if the staff would rise to the challenge and take charge, returning order and safety. Or would Rafael succeed in his use of aggression for power and control over adults? Would the adults show strength or weakness?

Suddenly, Rafael roared contemptuously, releasing his imprecations and wrath upon the world. "Fuck you, mothafuckas. I'm gonna bust y'al's heads!"

In a firm, direct voice, I command Rafael to release the chair, but he only replied with further invectives.

Obviously the teachers had spoken to him earlier with soft reason but to no avail. Six more staff members arrived, and the time had come to cross the ultimate threshold—physical restraint—because only action can bring equilibrium. Any delay in action now would only increase danger and chaos.

I moved toward Rafael while, to my right and rear, other staff moved forward. Without speaking, we united as one mind. Suddenly, Rafael moved to swing the chair, but I grabbed it while four male staff surged forward and seized Rafael. Bodies collided and thrashed, and heavy breathing filled the air. After I discarded the chair, I grabbed Rafael's arm—always an awkward and dangerous moment. Crossing this threshold seemed surreal and created an ethical quandary since we had infringed on a student's body space, but no option existed—we had to lean toward the light. Mr. Bosky and I each grabbed hold of one of Rafael's arms and got him in a controlled position. Takedowns rarely transpire as the smooth technique we learned when trained. My arms strained to manage Rafael's enormous strength, which was powered by adrenaline. Abruptly, he broke loose and threw an elbow into my ribs. He elbowed another staff member and kicked a third. Finally, we took him down to the floor and grabbed his wrists, locking him into a physically restrained position.

The staff maintained silence until Rafael calmed down, yet we periodically tell him that he needed to be calm before we would release him. We scanned Rafael to ensure the restraint wasn't excessive. Suddenly, silence reigns. Only the sound of heavy breathing filled the air. Perspiration and saliva dripped from Rafael's flushed red face. Fatigue and the odor of sweat soaked the air. The staff collaborated with furtive glances and dazed expressions, as if shell-shocked after a military bombardment. *Is this real?* We silently asked each other. *What the hell happened?* Moreover, we sought to determine if everyone remained injury free and to acknowledge this mutual experience—the bizarreness, the stress, and the horror.

As we waited for Rafael to completely relax, he suddenly burst out a shrieking cry that expressed a medley of frustration, rage, and pain. I knew this voice because it manifested the inner soul beneath the mask of aggression. The shriek reverberated like a mourning elegy from the nadir of the human soul, where darkness, rage, grief, and pain reside. One never gets used to this ominous voice because it evokes apprehension, fear, and sorrow. But we, the staff, unite with these youth, not only in their light but also in their darkness. Our physical control of the student equated with a human embrace that conveyed, *We fear you not; we stand with you in light and darkness.*

Children of Darkness

This experience with Rafael, although quite rare and extreme, provides an opportunity to examine and better understand aggressive behavior both within adolescents and in ourselves. In this section, I will present information about aggressive behavior. *What are the behavioral signs that someone might be prone to become violent? What are the risk factors that push people over the edge? How can we avoid a possible violent situation? What occurs in the brain when someone becomes agitated?*

One sign that suggests a student might act out violently is when his or her actions seem aimed at intimidating and evoking fear in students or staff. The student may make implied verbal threats or construct hypothetical situations of possible threats. She may ask, "What would you do if I punched you in the face?" In addition, the student body has an intuitive sense about an aggressive student. You'll notice that, generally, students will shy away from the potential aggressor; however, some students—dependent types— might gravitate to him out of fear and want to befriend him to feel protected and experience vicariously his "power." But the most important method staff members can use to look for signs that a student may become violent is through direct communication with the individual. *After days and weeks, is the student capable of forming a rapport with the staff? Is the student detached emotionally? Does he or she give the staff an eerie instinctive sense of behavioral unpredictability and possible explosive rage?* Get feedback from other staff to determine their sense of the youth. The staff's "intuition"— emotional intelligence—about the student is the cornerstone for an accurate appraisal. If the staff reaches a consensus that there is reason to be concerned, then the next step would be to communicate with the caregiver. Doing so will give you a bigger picture; you'll learn how the student behaves and interacts at home and get information as to whether he or she may possibly be involved with other risk factors, such as truancy or the criminal justice system. You might determine whether there are any counselors, truancy, or probation officers involved who could provide additional information. Other risk factors include a broken family structure or single-parent family, excessive geographical and school mobility—that is, living for short stays with various relatives, communities, schools, groups, and foster homes—juvenile detention, or the youth being a ward of the state due to physical or sexual abuse or neglect.

The most important factor in avoiding a possible violent situation is to build an ongoing relationship with the student. If a basic sense of trust and respect can be established, then the staff can have some influence to persuade the student to calm down in a volatile situation. All staff should be informed about a student staff members are concerned about and be prepared to act according to the school's crisis intervention plan. Staff should avoid personal power struggles and talk to the student about the disciplinary consequences of violent behavior, such as school suspension, expulsion, and law enforcement. Often, aggressive students will act out violently in school to self-sabotage because they don't want to be there; they may want to quit school or even return to juvenile detention because they fear making independent choices, taking responsibility, and forming meaningful relationships. As a result, often the student unconsciously orchestrates a violent scenario to compel the staff to decide her or his fate—*It's not my fault; the school threw me out.*

Over many years of similar experiences with youth like Rafael, in my mind, these situations always beckoned the question, what is the purpose of Rafael's behavior? Clearly, Rafael knew beforehand how the staff would respond. Often with students like Rafael, the staff observed these patterns of self-sabotaging behavior. This question often dominated my thinking and had always compelled me to seek to understand this mystery and the purpose of such self-destructive behavior. Below, I will begin to explore this theme, a central subtext to this book.

The situation illustrates what author Konrad Lorenz (1969, 47) found in his research on aggression—that the real danger rests not with aggression per se but with its obscure *spontaneity*, that is, when it arises by chance or out of the blue, as it did for Rafael on this calm morning. Neuroscientists have discovered exactly what happens in the brain with aggressive behavior. Researchers have identified the amygdala in the limbic brain as the focal point for fear and the storage space of emotional memory for self-preservation purposes (Goleman 1996, 341–43). Thus, the amygdala is like the central command center that initiates the autonomic nervous system's fight-or-flight response. In short, psychologist Daniel Goleman (19—20) called the amygdala an internal alarm system that can overrun the brain's neocortex despite its reason and logic. In his classic book, *On Aggression*, Lorenz (1969, 47) concurred with Freud that there exist two central risk factors that predispose individuals toward violent aggression—the lack of meaningful relationships and, most importantly, the deprivation of human love.

In the same vein, psychoanalyst Erich Fromm (1964, 23, 30) wrote that sociopaths have adapted a character "orientation" toward the "love of death and destruction." Violence becomes a replacement for authentic self-power and the capacity to love and to work. Usually a sociopath will embrace guns and weapons as symbols of power and destruction. Fromm (31) maintained that the sociopath seeks to have *"revenge on life for negating itself to him."* I sense this sociopathic motive toward revenge and negation relates to the person's deep inferiority, which he or she denies and acts out with an attitude of superiority through aggression. Fromm (33) summed that the only cure for a sociopath resides in the development of his or her creative powers and potentiality.

These scholars stressed the need for love, which is the quintessential humanizing force of life. In short, whether as a parent, educator, or counselor, the essence of life and work rests in the simple yet crucial relationship building and cultivating the relationship with a child like a garden throughout his or her childhood. But adolescents like Rafael, due to abuse and neglect during childhood, fear emotional closeness with anyone. Their experience tells them it will only lead to further abuse, neglect, or abandonment. Therefore, Rafael exemplifies the consequences of the deprivation of love, nurture, and a healthy culture. As a result, this group of children and youth are some of the most difficult to treat and work with, and yet the only treatment for them is what authors Lorenz, Freud, and Fromm recommended—to love and to work.

I sensed that Rafael's violent episode was a symbolic reenactment of his past, which included a severe physically abusive and violent upbringing. Rafael was among the myriad of youth whom I refer to as the *children of darkness*, whose behavior leads them into the crime, violence, and the dark abyss of prisons. These children of darkness want to impose their violent retribution on a seemingly unjust and unloving world. Their crying voices radiate a ubiquitous, silent melody of sorrow and pain that echoes incessantly upon the earth. But we usually become mute to this sound because it creates such poignant anguish and horror. It seems that we only hear their real voices when we cross life's invisible thresholds, as we did with Rafael. Yet with adolescents like Rafael, I seek their darkness. I don't know why, but I seek their darkness as someone who seeks for light in the dark.

Someone on the staff phoned the police, who later arrested Rafael for assault. Two days later, Rafael returned to Cougarville. About four weeks after that, police arrested Rafael again, this time for burglary. This infraction violated his parole, so he returned to prison. The behavior of students like Rafael conveys their subconscious intention to self-destruct and be imprisoned. It seems irrational—who would want to live in prison? But Rafael fears change, responsibility, and the quest to discover a new social role or identity, such as a laborer or carpenter. Entrapped by fear, Rafael has encased himself in the pseudosecurity of the false identity as a gangbanger.

Rafael's self-destructive behavior displays the unconscious dynamism of the internal self-destroyer/saboteur—a ubiquitous and powerful force (see chapters 14 and 17). The traumas of abuse, neglect, and abandonment, along with illiteracy, usually produce deep feelings of inferiority and self-hate. The self-saboteur or self-destroyer within dominates these children of darkness. The self-destroyer within us is a major subtext in this book. What is this darkness inside Rafael and all of us? What is this force inside us that can suddenly be unleashed to destroy?

The Dark Monster in the Unconscious: The Pain of Life

I believe parents and educators may find two aspects of this encounter with Rafael quite useful. Though the situation with Rafael was rare, it has been my experience that the most difficult youth have been the most beneficial to me in my personal and professional growth. On the one hand, the experience compelled me to embrace, manage, and utilize my aggressive instincts and intuition on a higher plane. The intensity of the situation compelled me to become more attuned inwardly with my aggressive instinct and use it constructively to manage and model the appropriate use of aggression. The principle that conflict can be a means for change and growth applies to any personal conflict, whether with one's child, spouse, or coworker. When we challenge and manage these aggressive behaviors or conflicts successfully, we often can perceive the real person behind the anger—a fearful, emotionally wounded individual who yearns for healing.

Second, our emotional relationships with family, friends, and fellow employees can sometimes become distressed with conflict and feelings of anger and hurt. Conflict proves inevitable in life. Everyone must take responsibility for his or her feelings and behaviors—even Rafael with his traumatized life. Although Rafael's is an extreme example, we can empathize with him. Some of us have experienced similar anger in our fantasies, in which we react aggressively to someone who offended us. However, we don't usually act it out because of internal controls, values, mores, and so forth. Sometimes we might feel like something is upsetting or irritating us within and we ask ourselves, *What is eating at me?* So whether it is an inner or outer conflict, the situation calls for action. We must find the root cause of the problem. Sometimes, what lurks beneath anger is emotional pain from an insult or memory from the past. This section will begin to present ways for teens or adults to increase their self-understanding so they can recognize what their emotions, such as anger, might be communicating in order to better manage conflict, decrease fears, and enhance healthy relationships. Simple methods will be presented to assist one to discover a greater sense of self-understanding, self-healing, and personal growth.

This encounter with Rafael is an example of when the monsters (in other words, the repressed pain of life) of the unconscious manifest in conscious reality—a nightmarish dream being acted out consciously.

Rafael's behavior reveals the contents of his unconscious—memories of childhood and the wounded child within.

In *East of Eden*, novelist John Steinbeck (2002, 131–32) described Cathy, who shot her husband and abandoned her two children in order to pursue her own self-interests in a house of prostitution:

> It doesn't matter that Cathy was what I have called a monster. Perhaps we can't understand Cathy, but on the other hand we are capable of many things in all directions, of great virtues and great sins. And who in his mind has not probed the dark waters? Maybe we all have in us a secret pond where evil and ugly things germinate and grow strong ... Might it not be that in the dark pools of some men the evil grows strong enough to wriggle over the fence and swim free? Would not such a man be our monster, and are we not related to him in our hidden water?

Steinbeck analyzed with acumen that whether for Cathy or Rafael, the human condition yields dark waters in the unconscious where the pain of life can transmogrify into a monster. We should probe our dark waters because our neurotic and problematic behaviors usually relate to the dark waters in the unconscious. Jung (1978, 8–9) called these dark waters or behavior the *shadow*—and everyone has shadows. A shadow composes that behavior others observe and don't like about us. We often have a blind spot for our shadows because it conceals the brat side in us—our infantile demands and inferiorities. When we encounter conflicts with others or lose our temper, those situations usually display a clue of the shadow in us and others. So we must work to eliminate our shadows by assessing our behaviors, attitudes, and motives. This awareness helps us to withhold critical judgment of others when we realize that beneath their improper behavior resides the fear of self-knowledge of their inner shadows and emotional wounds. Our shadow behaviors are often simply maladaptive ways for us to overprotect the wounded child within us. (To learn more about a way to explore one's shadows, and to increase self-understanding and self-power, and if necessary, seek the advice of a counselor, see chapter 12, "A Sacred Place." To learn more about a technique to cleanse one's emotional baggage, see "Recapitulation" in chapter 13.)

Rafael rages for a reason, and his behavior manifests a purpose and rationality. He seeks to destroy his pain of life in order to be healed and free—a death and rebirth. He relentlessly vents his anger upon the world because he fears the painful emotional wounds and the difficult act of purging. Jung (1989, 250) held that a neurosis, a mental and emotional disorder, manifests *"as an act of adaptation that has failed"* and accordingly, he thought this analysis could implicitly merge with "Freud's view that a neurosis is, in a sense, an attempt at self-cure—a view which can be and has been applied to many other illnesses." Although Jung and Freud meant physical illness in this context, I sense that neurosis as "self-cure" holds true for most of our maladaptive behaviors, whether alcohol and drug abuse, sexual acting out, or acts of violence.

With accurate analysis and language, we can understand Rafael's unconscious behavior, the subterranean world of the seemingly irrational. The seemingly irrational behavior usually makes rational sense. So with Rafael, I must quickly *perceive* beyond the visible rage into the invisible plane of his past and view his behavior as symbolic—as metaphorical. The German writer Johann Wolfgang von Goethe said (quoted in Patillo and Manchi 1988) that "all things are metaphors." Mythology refers to Rafael's behavior of rage as the realm of the *underworld*, where monsters and boon reside. Psychology calls this the unconscious—the reservoir of memories and the abode of aggressive and sexual energies and drives. This raging beast-monster must be faced, challenged, and purged. If avoided, unchecked, and feared, this dormant beast-monster will possibly be a harbinger of violence, rape, death, and self-destruction.

Rafael's behavior reveals a reenactment of his traumatized past or *pain of life*. His behavior resembles a metaphor and a recapitulation of his life history. On the one hand, Rafael wants to *destroy* something because of his pain; on the other hand, he wants the pain extinguished. But in this vain attempt to eliminate the pain, he inadvertently seeks to destroy others—the projected objects or people that wounded him in the past. Rafael wishes to be healed; he seeks a sense of release, harmony, and wholeness, but he does not know how to heal himself. Jung (1990a, 388) upheld that humans possess an instinctive impulse and urge for self-healing. Jung used the circle or mandala (which means "a circle" in Sanskrit) as a pedagogical and therapeutic device with patients. In fact, Jung maintained that the circle exists as the most powerful of symbols (Campbell in Patillo and Manchi 1988) and even Plato, in the *Timaeus*, referred to the soul as a sphere (Jung 1978, 136). The reason rests in the circle's universal experience, such as with time; the seasons of the year; and the shapes of the embryo, earth, moon, sun, and so forth. Jung (1990a, 388) interpreted schizophrenic patients' use of the circle (wholeness) in drawings, dreams, or visual hallucinations as, "An *attempt at self-healing* on the part of Nature, which does not spring from conscious reflection but from an instinctive impulse." Therefore, most behavior can be viewed metaphorically as a means to restore psychic balance, wholeness, and self-healing.

For Rafael, metaphorically speaking, something did need to be destroyed or to die. What was needed was not the murder of others or the turning in upon the self as in suicide but rather, he needed to exterminate the wounds of the past. (In chapter 9, we'll examine the fictional character, Ebenezer Scrooge, who did just that.) Rafael perpetuates his pain by not facing his past and letting it go. Rafael seeks to be released, but he only learned to act out aggressively for a sense of resolution and relief. I sense that, deep within students like Rafael, they want the light of life. But they remain afraid, and fear dominates them. Hence, they become entrapped in the darkness of pain, anger, and hate. Yet perplexed teens like Rafael unconsciously act out the source of their pain as if it were a nightmarish dream. For most of us, the source of our pain lies in the past of childhood, and extinguishing these ghosts of the past seems like an impossible dream.

Key Points

- Caregivers must challenge aggressive behavior to maintain a safe environment. Beneath the mask of aggression, youth are confronting issues of fear, anger, inferiority, and identity.

- Neuroscience research shows that the amygdala is the brain's center for fear and emotional memory—the emotional brain—and with excessive stress it can overrule the rational mind. Therefore, aggression is at its most dangerous level when it arises spontaneously.

- Behavioral signs of a potentially violent student include frequent use of intimidation, verbal threats, and emotional detachment; the staff's inner voice or "intuition" rests as the central measure for an accurate assessment of a potential violent outburst. The primary risk factors for a potentially violent person are the denial of love from caregivers and the absence of healthy relationships; therefore, youth who become wards of the state due to physical and sexual abuse and neglect or who are sentenced to juvenile detention tend to be high risk.

- The staff's most effective means of avoiding violent behavior is through maintaining ongoing relationships with each student. A relationship that possesses a sense of basic trust and respect can be highly beneficial in a volatile situation and can enable the de-escalation of behaviors. All staff should be aware of a potentially violent student and be ready to respond in accord with the school's crisis intervention plan.

- Aggressive situations provide an opportunity to learn more about one's own aggressive drives and how to use this powerful force constructively in the management of volatile situations. In conflict always resides the potential for learning and personal growth. Often, behind the mask of violent aggression rests an individual trapped in fear, emotional pain, and an unfulfilled longing for healing.

- Everyone has pitfalls or "shadows" that make up our inferiorities. Often our shadows manifest when we are in irritable moods or during personal conflicts with others. Usually, our shadow behaviors like anger are simply a maladaptive way for us to shield the wounded child within us. Examining and acknowledging our shadows will bring release from their negative effect in our lives.

- Acting out behavior can be viewed "metaphorically" as a symbolic psychological reference to one's past history; traumatized individuals often develop a negative self-concept of inferiority and self-hate; consequently, they tend to act out in a pattern of self-sabotaging behaviors.

- Psychological research shows that all behaviors are adaptive with the unconscious intent to sooth and bring self-healing. Therefore, maladaptive behaviors— like alcohol or drug abuse and acting out sexually or violently—compose our inborn instinctive attempts to self-heal.

SIX

The "Rebirth" of Charles

On a September morning in 1997 at Cougarville, I received a notice about a meeting on a new student. When I read the name, Charles Brown, my heart sunk. Anxiety and terror jetted up my spine. I had feared that Charles, who had attended Cougarville five years earlier, would return some day. The memory of the day Charles's misbehavior escalated into a fit of psychotic rage and compelled staff to physically restrain him haunted me. While I, along with at least four other staff members, held him down, Charles had literally bucked me off him like a horse in a rodeo—and this had occurred when Charles was only ten. He was the size of a fourteen-year-old then, so how big and wild would he be now? I had always repressed my concerns about his return, but deep inside I had known he would be back. Charles epitomized my deepest unconscious fear on the job—the "uncontrollable" youth. Now I had to face this fear, which would become one of the biggest challenges of my career.

As I sat at the large, oblong table in the conference room with five other staff members, I heard a loud bass voice echo from the hallway—my anxiety and dread increased. Suddenly, out of the dark hallway, a huge creature emerged and swaggered cockily into the room. In a loud, boisterous voice, he bellowed, "What's up, man?" Charles wore a baseball cap—cocked to the side, gangbang style—and dressed in baggy pants and shirt, but he now stood six foot four and weighed 340 pounds, without an ounce of fat! My nightmare had become a reality, and immediately, I launched a myriad of prayers to the Heavens. *Why God? Why are you doing this to me? What did I do wrong to get this punishment? I don't deserve this nightmare.*

I think that maybe God responded with something like, *Why not? You think you're so good in your craft, and besides you act a bit cocky so stop whining and accept the challenge.*

Along with Charles were his father and stepmother, Mr. and Mrs. Brown, and his Illinois state caseworker, Mr. Jones. After formal introductions transpired, Mr. Jones briefed us that, in the other school, Charles had bullied, threatened students and teachers, intimidated staff, refused to do any class work, and walked out of the school any time he desired; in short, Charles had ruled supreme. Mr. Jones stressed that he aspired for Charles to attend Cougarville because he confidently knew that we would not allow Charles to behave in that manner. *Gee, thanks, Mr. Jones*, I thought. *Those words flow easy for you, especially if you don't have to challenge or physically restrain a beast like Charles.*

But Mr. Jones spoke truthfully because Cougarville maintained a reputation for managing the most difficult students in the county.

Charles had left Cougarville in 1992 because he had become a ward of the state. Years earlier, his mother had been admitted to a mental institution for psychiatric reasons. Charles and his two brothers lived with their grandmother, and their father remained uninvolved. Although the three boys went to school at Cougarville, their grandmother could not manage them because of their enormous emotional needs. Eventually, the state maintained custody of the boys.

In 1997, Charles's father remarried and reunited with his sons.

During the initial meeting with the parents, I immediately sensed that the key for Charles's success resided with his stepmother, a compassionate, kind, assertive, and strong woman. She loved Charles, and he displayed a strong attachment to her—he listened and obeyed her. She would become the strongest parent that I ever encountered in my twenty-two years of working with youth. There exists not a more difficult position in the world than a stepparent because, for any child, no one can ever replace his or her biological parents. Consequently, stepparents often become objects of rage for the stepchildren because of their intense loss, abandonment, and pain.

Charles's IQ tested at 68—borderline retarded. Everybody must be somebody and cling to an identity or social role. So Charles utilized his physical size, the gangbang facade, bullying, and intimidation for a sense of power and identity. Anyone would loathe the stigma of being labeled or identified as retarded or illiterate and might naturally relish an alternative identity, such as a gangbanger.

It did not take much time for Charles to start trouble. One morning as the staff waited at the entrance for the arrival of students' buses, the PA system announced an emergency "I-team" (intervention team) call. This meant that an urgent situation had arisen with an out-of-control student or fight, so a team of staff needed to meet the incoming bus. Therefore, about eight staff assembled, commandeered by our "main man," Mr. Rockwell. Mr. Rockwell measured in at six foot three and weighed three hundred pounds. He wore his long, blond hair in a braided ponytail and dressed in blue jeans and dress shirt with sleeves rolled up showing the tattoos on both his forearms.

The minivan bus pulled in and stopped. The door swung open, and Mr. Rockwell stood at the base of the door. "What's the problem?" he asked.

Suddenly, Charles lunged out of the bus onto Mr. Rockwell and began choking him with his hands. Mr. Rockwell's eyeballs bulged outwardly, as if they would pop out of their sockets.

Bedlam ensued. We rolled and thrashed around the parking lot. I felt like a cowboy who had fallen off of a bull with one hand still caught in the stirrups while being dragged around mercilessly. Finally, we pinned Charles down on the pavement. Six staff stacked on Charles like a bunch of lions on top of a water buffalo. His size made other physical restraint techniques obsolete. We called the police, and of course the rare time when we definitely need these guys, it took them thirty minutes to arrive.

Cougarville did not employ security guards so if serious trouble occurred with an aggressive student, the teacher didn't call the principal or the police. The teacher maintained authority and called an I-team for assistance. But on days like this, I deliberated with myself. *They don't pay me enough to deal with this madness. I may need to think about a different job.* Too many days like this one, and I'd resign because of excessive stress. I called that school year "the September of hell" because staff had to challenge five other rough students that month. Staff fatigue and burnout infected us as if the end of the school year had arrived, but it had only just started.

To make a long story short, Mr. Rockwell cruised to the hospital because of a heart condition, and Charles trekked to jail for assault. Yes, the situation demanded that Charles be taught a lesson, but of course, to my dismay, Charles returned.

Like most students, Charles challenged and tested the strength of the staff and program, but after this incident, he also joined the student body, where he fit in socially and prospered in Cougarville with impeccable attendance. So with parental support and a masterful teacher, Mr. Bosky, and his assistant, Mr. Rockwell, who provided a unique mishmash of timely attention, structure, and bellyaching humor, Charles thrived socially. Three years later, during Charles's senior year, debate arose among the staff whether Charles could ever manage a job. I felt strongly that he could work because my experience conveyed that when a teen experiences emotional or behavior problems, 99 percent of the time, the cause rests in the fact he or she chooses not to obtain a job and move toward responsibility and independence.

Eventually, Charles participated in the work-study program and acquired a part-time job in a drug store doing general maintenance and stock work. Charles relished the job, and his self-confidence blossomed. After Charles worked in the morning, he would return to school and he always strolled in with a bright smile while he hummed a song with aplomb. He was a big shot on top of the world, not a gangbanger with an attitude. He radiated self-mastery and independence. Charles silently sang the words of author and teacher Frank McCourt after McCourt had received his first salary as a teen. McCourt (1997, 396) observed people on the street and soliloquized, "I want them to know I'm like them, I'm a man ... I want to wave my pound note at the world so they'll say, There he goes Frankie McCourt [Charles Brown] the workingman, with a pound in his pocket."

Charles engaged in meaningful relationships and a job—in short, he *loved* and *worked*. Maslow (1982) wrote that human growth centers on the *thrill of* mastery (in other words, *peak experiences*)— whether mastery of carpentry, computer science, or maintenance worker skills. Charles and his parents glowed with pride on the day he graduated from high school—a fulfillment of a seemingly impossible dream. So in the end, Charles the beast transformed into a prince, and Charles stood victorious, having completed his adolescent tasks of education, responsibility, and independence.

Charles demonstrated the heroic path of self-transformation and exemplified the archetypal model for us. In 1997, Charles had identified as the tough gangbanger, but he courageously let go of the false social role that covered his fear to love and to succeed. Therefore, he experienced the death of the old self and a rebirth or resurrection toward authentic identity and self-power.

Author's Suggestions for Parents and Educators with a Difficult Child

In the early '90s during my first two years at Cougarville, the job was wrought with relentless anxiety and frustration; the program did not create a positive, healthy culture, and students consistently acted out, while the staff suffered internal conflict and division as a group. Actually, I seriously considered seeking employment elsewhere, but I endured this ordeal. In the meantime, I did extensive research on psychological treatment for adolescents with behavioral problems. One theme, one consensus among the experts remained constant— inspire and move teens through the tasks of adolescence. That is, help them move toward increased responsibility, independence, mastery of the "emotional" three Rs, a job, and so forth. So the suggestion sections in chapter 1 reflect this research; and my experiences at Cougarville, like the one with Charles, show how this approach can bear fruit. Therefore, along with the recommendations in chapter 1, I suggest three other actions in dealing with a difficult child:

1. Parents and teachers must stand as a united front.
2. Tighten discipline at home.
3. Incorporate creative programming at school.

Stand as a United Front

Eventually, with hard work and persistence at Cougarville, the staff developed a team mind-set. We learned to stand as a unified front. This front is the foundation for any coparents or educators dealing with a difficult child. Otherwise, youth will sense a division between adults in the home or school and, consequently, they'll tend not to feel safe and act out. Children may also take advantage of the division and manipulate caregivers, playing parents or educators against each other.

In the same vein, parents and educators need to work together as a united front on the student's behavioral and academic problems and goals. In a school conference, a parent can be supportive of his or her child and simultaneously stress the importance of the child's responsibility for behavior and schooling. In a parent conference with a problem student, I believe it is crucial to identify the specific problem behaviors that are the presenting problem, such as disruptive behavior or not completing classroom assignments. The trick then is to relate these behaviors to adolescent psychology as possible acts of avoidance, dependency, self-sabotage, and fear of independence (see chapter 1); this information, if used strategically and in a timely manner with the objective of aiding the adolescent's independence and academic success, gives parents and educators enormous psychological leverage. In general, the youth does not want to hear this direct, accurate appraisal, especially if his or her psychological cover or social mask is that of a tough rebel; the information usually evokes anxiety in youth, and he or she often responds defensively with denial and anger. Tactically, your intention should be to spark a small degree of anxiety in the youth; you don't want adolescents who are acting out to be comfortable in a situation that does not expect or demand accountability. Just like the athlete in competition or soldier in battle, these students need some anxiety as a source of energy to perform the necessary tasks or feats.

Moreover, when standing united with fellow caregivers and demanding responsibility, you are implicitly communicating to the youth that you know the real cause of his or her problem. You are clearly saying that if he or she doesn't move forward toward responsibility, you will again point out the real issues of dependency, irresponsibility, and the like. When the responsibility is put on the youth, parents and educators can feel free of the burden of guilt. Teens are not weak, and they can become responsible and independent. Often under the mask of bravado lie fear, self-doubt, and feelings of inferiority. Teens simply need the soft hand of compassionate support and the firm hand that demands accountability, responsibility, and emotional maturity in order to move forward in their personal growth and education.

At Home: Tighten Discipline

First, parents with a difficult child need to consistently tighten the reins of discipline—tough love. At Cougarville, sometimes a new teacher's classroom would be loud and unruly while the rest of the classrooms were quiet. Often the new teacher would surmise that he had the most troublesome students, but to his surprise, we would inform him they were all the same. Then the principal would simply inform the teacher to "tighten up" the discipline. Use every possible privilege item for leverage and impose logical consequences (see Dinkmeyer et al. 1998). Consequences might include limitations on cell phone usage and TV and computer access, withholding of allowance, room restriction, disallowing visitors, grounding, and so forth.

For example, if your son refuses to do homework or attend school, then you can ground him; if he refuses and leaves the house, then take other privileges away. If discipline has been too lax, discipline, particularly for youth between the ages of fifteen and seventeen, will be hard work. Initially, they will likely resist, and the road might be rocky for a while. But if you maintain consistency, not only will this discipline prove effective, your relationship with your teen will improve, with increased respect and communication, and you will become a stronger and more confident parent.

If the youth is sixteen or older and wants spending money, I suggest that he or she find a job. For some uncooperative teens, I have suggested to parents that they inform their teen that, if he or she is not working or in school, at age eighteen he or she will need to move out of the house. We must use leverage and mean it; teens instinctively know if we don't have the backbone to enforce rules, and then they won't respect the adult. The stipulation of moving out at age eighteen proves an effective tactical measure and usually creates appropriate anxiety for the teen to get moving toward responsibility and independence in their life.

I suggest that parents communicate consistently the concepts of adolescent psychology as noted above and in chapter 1, for example regularly using the key words of responsibility, accountability, and independence. And if your teen acts irresponsibly, then you can relate these behaviors to adolescent psychology as possible acts of avoidance, dependency, self-sabotage, and fear of independence. This basic knowledge of adolescent psychology from chapter 1 is parents' and educators' psychological suit of arms, allowing them to understand, to help, and to challenge problematic youth to move forward successfully.

Finally, you can watch with your teenager documentaries like *Scared Straight*, which is about a youth program for troubled teens who visit a prison for a day to observe and experience the realities of prison life. The visit provides a clear look at realistic consequences for irresponsibility and crime. Films like this were part of my instruction for adolescent students at Cougarville, and they always watched attentively.

In addition, wilderness experiences programs such as Outward Bound are highly successful with difficult youth. These outdoor adventure programs take a group of adolescents into nature for three to seven days to experience cooperative learning and teamwork through group living. Activities include camping, cooking, obstacle courses, repelling, hiking, rafting, canoeing, and enacting "solos" where each participant camps alone but within earshot of the adult leaders. In fact, Outward Bound has a program for at-risk youth and troubled teens. This experience moves youth away from their environment and families in order to offer them an experience where they might increase their awareness and independence and learn to handle the challenges of responsibility. Outward Bound accepts youth ages twelve to seventeen and young adults ages eighteen to twenty; scholarships are available, and participants can earn high school and college credits. (For more information on Outward Bound, visit the organization's website located at http://www.outwardbound.org/.)

One year at Cougarville an excellent teacher, Mr. Miller, took a group of five male adolescents for one full week to the adventure program linked with Southern Illinois University, and the experience proved highly successful for everyone. These programs can be costly, but grants are available, which is how Cougarville funded the trip, or donations could be procured from one's local business community. In addition, local urban outdoor programs do one-day team-building courses for groups like schools. Also some states have set up adolescent boot camps that offer similar types of programs. State universities appear to have these wilderness programs as well. So simply do an Internet search to find what's available.

At School: Implement Creative Programming

I believe that, often, the difficult student is communicating that the regular school setting does not fulfill his or her needs socially or academically—these students feel like they don't fit in. Furthermore, sometimes a full day of school proves too demanding on these types of students. Cougarville had a shortened day from 7:45 a.m. until 1:00 p.m., which is standard for most day schools for special education or behavior disordered students. I have visited alternative schools that had the similar half-day structure. A half day of school, along with a job in a work-study program, is highly recommended for difficult students. This formula decreases pressure and creates an environment in which the student can move toward independence.

Keep in mind, as we noted in chapter 1, Jung (1991, 56–57) emphasized that the most important function of schools is not in teaching knowledge but in producing independent individuals who are separate from their families.

Enrollment in a GED course is a viable option for a student at age seventeen who has the intelligence to pass the exam; this option is particularly valuable if the student lurks behind substantially in academic credits.

Finally, I think it proves important to ask the student to make a verbal commitment to her parents and educators that she will take responsibility for her education program and will make a *bona fide* effort to succeed.

In conclusion, this transfiguration of Charles from the possible fate of a violent descent into the dark abyss of prison or a mental institution to the ascent of human potentiality and radiance resembles the stories of myth and literature. Professor Campbell (1973, 257–58) wrote,

> And so, to grasp the full value of the mythological figures [whether Hercules or Charles] that have come down to us, we must understand that they are not only symptoms of the unconscious (as indeed are all human thoughts and acts) but also controlled and intended statements of certain spiritual principles, which have remained as constant throughout the course of human history as the form and nervous structure of the human physique itself. Briefly formulated, the universal doctrine teaches that all the visible structures of the world— all things and beings—are the effects of a ubiquitous power out of which they rise, which supports and fills them during

the period of their manifestation, and back into which they must ultimately dissolve. This is the power known to science as energy, to the Melanesian as *mana*, to the Sioux Indians as *wakonda*, the Hindus as *shakti*, and the Christians as the power of God. Its manifestation in the psyche is termed, by the psychoanalysts, *libido*. And its manifestation in the cosmos is the structure and flux of the universe itself.

Key Points

- Relationship building, literacy, and a job prove indispensable for human growth and development. Human nature yearns to love and work.
- Frequently, aggressive and bizarre behaviors mask feelings of inferiority or the fear of responsibility and independence and provide an alternative social role, albeit, an antisocial one.
- When parents and school staff work together toward the student's growth, responsibility, and independence, a magical dream can happen.
- Psychological research shows that effective treatment for "problematic" teens should center on movement toward responsibility and independence—the tasks of adolescence.
- With a difficult teen, use your suit of armor. Communicate about adolescent psychology consistently, stressing words like *responsibility, accountability,* and *independence*. Firm, fair, and consistent discipline—tough love—proves effective.
- With a difficult child, parents and educators need to work together as a united front on the student's behavioral and academic problems and goals.
- Proven effective programs for difficult teens include wilderness programs like Outward Bound and creative school programming like a half day of school and a job in a work-study program.

SEVEN

Kurt and the Internal Monster

This story reveals an episode of extreme rage by a young boy named Kurt whose acting-out behavior disclosed metaphorically the cause of his rage and pain of life. Like Rafael had, Kurt displayed the dangerous aspect of aggression—its spontaneity. In contrast to Rafael, Kurt was younger, had loving caregivers, and experienced early intervention from the school system. These combined factors significantly improved Kurt's chances for a successful adolescence and adulthood. As Freud, Lorenz, and Fromm (see chapter 5) emphasized, for humans to steer away from a life of violence, they need the early experience of human love, genuine relationships, and development of one's creative potentiality.

Kurt, a ten-year-old student, had a gentle, affable demeanor. He was a sweet boy who anyone would want as a brother or son. Kurt glowed. He was handsome, and impeccably attired, had dark brown eyes, and sported a butch type haircut. He lived with his aunt and uncle, who displayed immense love and care for him, and I sensed that Kurt knew this too. I engaged in play therapy, teaching children how to play appropriately (healthy play reflects healthy kids) weekly with students Kurt's age. Kurt always played army. He wore an army hat and constructed an elaborate fort and army base. Symbolically, the army play sustained him, giving him the sense of order, control, and protection that he needed in his life. When Kurt successfully left Cougarville, I gave him the army hat that he'd always worn in the playroom. Although it was just some old hat, Kurt smiled from ear to ear as if he'd received a Christmas present. The hat functioned as a "transitional object" for a memory of the healthy play, internal controls, and relationships he had established. During this time at Cougarville, Kurt presented himself as a model student, but I instinctively sensed serious problems existed. I observed this in his withdrawn eyes, for they conveyed dormant ghosts within. Indeed, his eyes mirrored the traumatized combat war veteran with PTSD whose "thousand-mile stare" seems to expand into infinity. I'm like an experienced auto mechanic; after years of experience I can diagnose problems by observation, experience, intuition, and instinct.

Suddenly one day, Kurt obstinately refused to do school assignments. As a consequence, he remained after school in a separate "time out" room to complete his schoolwork. The honeymoon ended, and the ghosts arose from the dark crevices of his mind. Thirty minutes later, Kurt's teacher, Mr. Washington, and I heard a shrieking scream. But this shriek differed from the typical temper tantrum cry, for it evoked an eerie poignancy. When we entered the room, we froze aghast. Kurt stood rigidly erect with tears pouring down his face, his eyes ablaze with a rage and hate that portended the urge to destroy and annihilate ad infinitum. Simultaneously, we perceived a pungent odor, and then we gasped in horror. Splattered on the walls and clutched in this little boy's hands was his fecal matter. Yes, this little boy felt like a worthless piece of "shit" because, in the past, someone had sexually violated his sacred anatomy. Kurt sought revenge, and he roared his aspiration to shit upon the world that had shat upon him. Kurt bled pain, and he wanted to destroy and annihilate to alleviate his pain of life—the shit of life. Kurt, like Rafael, acted out the wish to extinguish his pain in order to become healed.

After this incident, I met with Mr. Roberts, Kurt's uncle to discuss Kurt's behavior. When I mentioned my suspicion that Kurt had been sexually abused, Mr. Roberts remarked that he and his wife had heard the same from a family member and so they suspected it themselves. I mentioned to Mr. Roberts that this issue might need to be addressed in counseling in the future, particularly when Kurt entered adolescence. Kurt succeeded in our program because he worked at establishing relationships via communication and play; moreover, he maintained healthy boundaries in relationships—an essential requirement for anyone who has been physically or sexually abused, as abuse victims have experienced the violation of their physical boundaries. Finally, Kurt mastered his age-appropriate tasks of schoolwork (the three academic Rs). In short, Kurt engaged in love and work.

Future Internal Work in Psychotherapy

In the future, Kurt will likely need to work through these abuse issues in psychotherapy because, at age ten, his brain physiology and thinking processes have not fully developed. Furthermore, he does not possess the necessary language to adequately process such abstract concepts such as sex abuse, sexuality, anger, pain, and revenge. Yet midadolescence, ages fifteen to seventeen, will provide Kurt an opportunity to engage in this internal work because, during this stage, intense emotions (joy, anxiety, love, affection, fears, insecurities, emotional pain, anger, and sadness) surge upon adolescents like a tidal wave—the great barrier—which might feel like an internal psychological war (see chapter 1). Moreover, the human brain changes physiologically. Teens can now think differently about abstract ideas, reasoning, logic, and critical thinking. Midadolescence entails a difficult adjustment for anyone, but for those who experienced severe past traumas, the adjustment tends to be more demanding. Due to Kurt's past abuse, these new thought processes and emotions would likely trigger painful memories, confusion, anger, insecurities, anxieties, and fears of his identity and sexuality. He might have a number of questions. *Was the sexual abuse my fault? Am I destined to become a sex abuser too? Should I seek violent revenge upon my offender? Am I a homosexual?*

A danger exists that he could become an abuser himself, as he might come to believe that the only way to resolve the trauma is to project his rage on someone else (see chapter 13). Furthermore, sex abuse or rape essentially *steals* the sexuality of the victim. His or her unique and sacred sexuality lies defiled and destroyed and needs to be renewed and reborn. Rapists and sex abusers probably experienced sex abuse themselves and seemingly perpetuate the cycle of abuse by the illusory unconscious attempt to regain their lost sexuality through aggressive sexual assault. Behavior can be viewed metaphorically as an attempt at self-healing or wholeness (see chapter 5).

Middle and late adolescence provides this opportunity to work through the problems or ghosts of childhood, such as abandonment, separation and loss from parental divorce and deaths, shame and doubt of one's abilities, mistrust of people and relationships, feelings of inferiority, self-hate, guilt, abuse and neglect, and emotional dependencies. Everyone experienced, to some degree, problem issues or ghosts from our childhood; no one escapes the pain of life.

During Kurt's adolescence, two treatment issues would likely emerge. First, as noted above, Kurt should thoroughly experience the full range of human emotions. Second, like Scrooge (see chapter 9), Kurt should undergo a therapeutic catharsis (in other words, a rite of purification) of his pain, anger and loss; that is, with language, he will need to identify his emotions of anger, hurt, loss, and so forth. The wounded boy will still lurk inside him, and he could develop self-protective behaviors, such as anger, aggression, isolation, intellectualizations, rationalizations, and so forth. He will also need to eject the image of the abuser in his psyche. The image of the abuser creates a false belief system, where the victims believe they have become worthless individuals because of this desecrating and traumatic experience (see chapters 12 and 13).

The cathartic purge would be important for Kurt because emotions operate as guides to experience the depth of our humanity as well as the unconscious, where answers lie dormant in our quest to discover self-knowledge. Jung (1990a, 335) stressed the importance of this psycho-emotional purge for liberation from past trauma. He wrote, "Real liberation comes not from glossing over or repressing painful states of feeling, but only from experiencing them to the full." Therefore, with guidance from a competent psychotherapist (see chapter 12)—Jung (1991, 62; 1985, 3) refers to such therapists as, *physicians of the soul in the healing art of psychotherapy*—one can eventually experience a degree of healing and emotional mastery and shout the words of writer Richard Wright (1993a, 424), "But I was a man now and master of my rage, able to control the surging emotions."

Key Points

- Abused children need loving caregivers and a supportive school to become successful in the future.
- The vast physical and psychological changes at midadolescence provides youth with the verbal and thinking capacity to better face, understand, and work through their problems like abuse, inferiority, or abandonment in psychological treatment.
- To become truly free and healed from past pain of life, one needs to emotionally experience and verbally express—a cathartic purge—the emotional wounds and upsets from the past.

EIGHT

Marcus and the Invisible Beast

Everyone has his or her own unique pain of life, and for some individuals, the cause rests in the stain of feeling inferior. Through this story, I aim to aid parents and educators in becoming more aware of this phenomenon and the pervasiveness of inferiority by examining the behavior of a young boy, Marcus, who makes a vain attempt at *self-cure* for his feelings of inferiority. As exhibited in previous chapters and stories, these methods of self-cure often include "quick fixes," "panaceas," or "self-medicating" ploys like alcohol and drug abuse, sexual acting out, acts of aggression intended to get power, revenge or attention seeking. Furthermore, as Jung noted (see chapter 5), we possess an instinct that seeks self-healing—to feel whole—as shown by Charles with his healthy actions of love and work or by Rafael's and Kurt's ineffective violent outbursts that sought a sense of release, wholeness, and resolution. In the story below, Marcus shared with me the pain of life that inflicts him and others like an incurable plague.

Therefore, in this chapter we will explore Marcus's pain of life and how feelings of inferiority can have a ripple effect of anxiety, fear, and aggression, which often compounds and reinforces the universal obstacle of fear that everyone must overcome during stages of separation and change in life such as adolescence. From years of research and experience, I have determined that this deep unconscious sense of inferiority and its concomitant—self-hatred— usually comprise the basis of one's emotional wounds or pain of life that often get acted out through self-sabotaging behaviors, outward aggression, or self-aggression. The heroic path of independence, self-change, and increased self-awareness (see part 3 and part 4) provides the means for victory over the false belief of inferiority, fear, and self-hate. My unbending intent is to bring the possibility of light, hope, self-understanding, and a means for genuine self-healing for children like Marcus.

Marcus, an eleven-year-old African American student, was a unique character. I nicknamed him, "the Emperor," because at the initial meeting in the conference room at Cougarville he sat unabashedly in a chair like an emperor on his throne. He obstinately refused to talk with the staff or even his mother. Marcus, arrayed with two homemade Indian ink tattoos on both forearms, glared with bellicosity and defiance. Marcus acted like the toughest dude in town. But like most students, Marcus had constructed a defensive front or social mask for self-protection, and over time, as I expected, he emerged as the sweet and sensitive kid that had lurked underneath the callous facade. During our counseling time in my office, we always played basketball with a miniature basketball hoop. We joked and laughed while we jostled competitively, and then Marcus always grinned from ear to ear after he dunked the basketball with authority. He always beat me in a real close game. Marcus's ebullience filled the air after he won the games. Marcus knew I always let him win, but we never talked about that; we knew that to win did not matter because our time together meant the essence of life—relationship.

Marcus succeeded in our program because we resolved his core problem behavior as "the Emperor" in the classroom, which manifested as fighting and cursing. The problem for Marcus, as was is for many students, involved illiteracy, and he required caring, yet strong discipline. Heck, if one doesn't get self-confidence or a sense of self-power in academics or athletics, then being the tough dude becomes the natural, adaptive behavior.

One day, as Marcus and I talked in my office, which we did before playing basketball, I noticed some dry, white spots on his arms. I advised to him to get some lotion for his dry skin because cold winter weather dries skin out. I will never forget the look in Marcus's innocent, round brown eyes. They suddenly conveyed a deep sorrow—his anguish and *pain of life*. Then Marcus spoke, "Sometimes when I take a bath I put bleach in the water."

His words pierced my heart. How should I respond? Of course, I said the natural thing. "You are a beautiful kid with beautiful skin."

Marcus's eyes turned downward, and he shook his head in the negative. The futility of my reply disturbed, panged, and angered me.

Marcus's behavior reflects, on a microcosm level, the manifestation of the scourge of rejection and inferiority that inflicts humanity like an incurable plague. Referring to the story of Cain and Abel, novelist John Steinbeck (2002, 268) wrote, "I think it is the symbol story of the human soul. ... The greatest terror a child can have is that he is not loved, and rejection is the hell he fears. I think everyone in the world to a large or small extent has felt rejection. And with rejection comes anger, and with anger some kind of crime in revenge for the rejection, and with the crime guilt—and there is the story of mankind."

Black inferiority and self-hatred emerged long ago. In the 1940s, writer Richard Wright (1993a, 298) described this psychological crisis of many African Americans. "I had seen many Negroes solve the problem of being black by transferring their hatred of themselves to others with black skin and fighting them."

Author V. S. Naipaul (1990, 50–51) wrote a social critique of the American South in *A Turn in the South*. Naipaul engaged in a discussion on race with Michael Lomax, a thirty-eight-year-old educated black politician and candidate for mayor of Atlanta in 1989. The black radical writer William Du Bois was Lomax's hero. Naipaul recounted this frank conversation below. Lomax explained:

The civil-rights movement distorted our conception of human relations. It made it completely adversarial. In an adversarial relationship there is a good person and a bad person, a victim and a victimizer. We were the good, we were the victim. None of the current black leaders talked of black responsibility, he said.

And yet for him, with all that he had become, and all his future, there was still the burden of being black. He spoke of the burden in this way (and he might have spoken the words often before): There's not a day, not a moment in my life when I don't have to think about the color of my skin. And being black is not just about what I see. It's about what I feel about myself. It's as much internal as external.

I think sometimes that an exorcism has got to happen for all of us, where you pull out all of those evil demons of race. They're still inside us, fighting with one another. ... You have to confront your own demons. For me it's confronting the fact that I am a black person and that every time a white person sees me I may be no different for him than seeing a drunk on the street. And that colors the way I think about myself. I have been angry about being black, saddened by it. And I cannot deal with the white person or the black person until I look in the mirror and accept the man I see there.

So Michael Lomax courageously revealed the burden and internal war that being black was for him and his desire for self-acceptance and liberation. Indeed, Lomax's deft perspicacity provided a solution for what children like Marcus need when he concluded, "Blacks had to look inwards. ... The need now was not for marches so much as for an internal revolution" (Naipaul, 1990, 50).

Marcus remained at Cougarville for about two years. After a six-month transition back into his district school, Marcus returned full-time. The home district school never reported any behavior problems throughout his elementary and high school years. So now

Marcus stood as the victorious emperor of his own palace—his unique, autonomous self. Thus, through learning to read with the help of a masterful teacher, Ms. Sobieski, and a school with structure and a positive culture, Marcus began a new path. Instead of using aggression for power, he experienced the ahas of peak experiences such as learning to read and, consequently, likely experiencing a genuine inner sense of self-power and self-healing. So, in a sense, Marcus took a giant step toward self-change and toward an internal revolution to eliminate his inferiority and build self-confidence through the experience of love and work.

The Triadic Scourge of Inferiority: Anxiety, Fear, and Aggression

Why did Marcus put bleach in his bath water? Everyone knows but most of us *fear* to mention *it*. Indeed, we mirror the marooned boys in William Golding's *Lord of the Flies* (1954, 52) who *feared* the snakelike beast. But the unsung hero, Simon, fearlessly crosses the threshold of fear and taboo and declares, "'As if ... the beastie or the snake-thing, was real. Remember?' The two older boys flinched when they heard the shameful syllable. Snakes were not mentioned now, were not mentionable."

So Simon courageously crossed the *threshold of fear* into the uncertain, anxiety-laden, and amorphous social construction of *taboo*—where reality appears uncertain, irrational, fearful, and unspeakable. Simon used emotionally explicit language to create clarification with the hope of nullifying the oppressive climate of fear manufactured by the newly established cultural myth—belief in the beast (whether the belief consists of inferiority, racial superiority, victimization, or any false ideology).

Simon realized that the beast existed only in the boys' imaginations, and it had evolved out of the *anxiety and fear of the unknown*. As Róheim (see chapter 4) stressed, the ubiquitous force of *anxiety* dominates cultures, and now the boys as a group manufactured their own subculture. Thus, anxiety and fear became the *tour de force* that sparked the boys into aggressive acts of murder; yes, *fear* awoke the monster within—the death instinct—to destroy.

Simon models the archetypal hero path for Marcus, Kurt, and all of us because of his strength, valor, confidence, and autonomy. Simon trusted his inner instincts and embraced the difficult emotions of rejection and fear. And in doing so, he enabled himself to plunge into deeper reflective thought, analysis, and resolution. Simon refused the traps of fear, false thinking, or beliefs of the group. He rejected the image of the beast (whether inferiority, victimhood, or anything else), and he visualized beyond the obstructions of fear and illusion. Like Simon, we must learn to identify the invisible, unknown sources of our anxieties and fears—usually something irrational. Yet for Marcus, Kurt, and all of us, there lie the dormant memories of the wounded child within us, who can be awoken like a sleeping dragon and who we will defend with a vengeance.

Later, Simon discovered the central problem during the group's volatile and anxiety-laden discussion that leaned toward refuting the existence of the beast. Simon allowed, "'Maybe, … maybe there is a beast.' The assembly cried out savagely. … 'What I mean is … maybe it's only us.' … Simon became inarticulate in his effort to express mankind's essential illness. Inspiration came to him."

Simon astutely articulated the book's central premise—that humanity's essential illness lies in the *projection* of our *fears* upon others. Projection functions as a psychological defense mechanism as when one attributes his or her feelings, thoughts, or attitudes onto other individuals or groups. Thus, our false beliefs and projections often lead to the triadic tandem and juggernaut of anxiety, fear, and aggression (either directed at others or at ourselves). Therefore, the core problem exists inside us.

John Steinbeck, a master in the psychology of literature, points out the universality of human fear of one another and how, thereby, fear is the main inward force that fuels projection on others and external acts of aggression. As noted in chapter 1, Freud discovered that the source of most psychological illness rests in fear of self-knowledge—of one's emotions, memories, potentialities, and so forth. If we fear to go *inward* toward self-discovery, then we inevitably project *outwardly* our fears on others. Moreover, often projection is simply a device to avoid and deny the unknown within us—particularly our shadow of inferiority (Jung 1978, 8–9).

In Steinbeck's *Of Mice and Men* (1978, 35), George described to Slim how he and Lennie traveled together. "Ain't many guys travel around together," he [Slim] mused. "I don't know why. Maybe ever'body in the whole damn world is scared of each other." I sense that *fear* and its frequent concomitant, *aggression*, often become ignited by a deeper sense of *self-hatred* (for example, the feeling of inferiority or castration fears, which is when one's masculinity or femininity becomes threatened or insecure). In Steinbeck's *In Dubious Battle* (2006, 253–54), two union organizers engaged in a conflict with the landowners who commanded aggressive vigilantes to thwart unionization. The two organizers plunged into the following dialogue:

"Well, a little loss of blood won't hurt me."

Mac stroked his lower lip nervously. "Jim," he said. "Did you ever see four or five dogs all fighting?"

"No."

"Well, if one of those dogs gets hurt or goes down, all the rest'll turn on him and kill him."

"So what?"

"So—men do that sometimes, too. I don't know why. It's kind of like Doc says to me one time, Men hate something in themselves."

Steinbeck suggested three quintessential characteristics of the darkness of human nature—fear of others, aggression, and self-hate. I think fear and self-hate (inferiority) compose ubiquitous psychological dynamics that spark acts of aggressive destruction.

Why? I sense we simply fear something inside ourselves that we unconsciously hate—the darkness (in other words, feelings of inferiority, shadows, past traumas, and the like). Yes, the darkness of our human nature can suddenly become a destructive force. Projection is the pathway or linkage point between the inner self (fear and self-hate) and outward behavior (aggression).

For an accurate psychological analysis, we must make overt what lies covert. That is, we must bring to the light of consciousness what exists in the dark unconscious (e.g., anxiety, fear, anger, loss, abandonment, abuse, or inferiority) because awareness extinguishes fear, anxiety, and false beliefs of inferiority or self-hate. Simon modeled this for us. Therefore, for Marcus, Kurt, and most of us, the existence of this invisible beast within often seems related either to a prevalent cultural taboo—a false myth—or to a personal experience such as rejection or failure that instills a false belief of inferiority.

Facing our inner wounds of inferiority takes a heroic effort, yet Charles, Kurt, and Marcus displayed that self-change can occur through loving relationships and peak experiences, in short, through loving and working. Yet, self-change is an ongoing process (see chapters 12, 13, and 15). Old ghosts from the past might reappear, and we must face the anxiety of new challenges. The next chapter will present the theme of growth, self-change, and self-healing by examining a literary character who models for us the courage to face the pain of life and take necessary actions toward self-change and happiness.

Key Points

- One's inner inferiorities and fears can be projected on people and spark anxiety, fear, and aggressive acting out externally toward others or turned inwardly on the individual himself.
- The emotional wounds or pain of life generally consist of one's unconscious inferiority and/or self-hate. Fear tends to maintain the false cultural beliefs like racial or gender inferiority or victimization. Through the activities of

self-examination, self-change, and independence, one can overcome his or her fears, feelings of inferiority, and self-hate.

- Self-change and self-knowledge come by becoming more aware of the unacknowledged contents in one's unconscious, including fears, anxieties, anger, abuse, and feelings of inferiority.

NINE

The Heroic Journey of Ebenezer Scrooge to Purge the Wounds of Christmas Past

So how do Marcus, Kurt, Rafael, or anyone else extinguish the haunting emotional wounds of the past? The means of doing so lie in the solitary, inward hero path as exemplified by the infamous literary character Ebenezer Scrooge. Indeed, Scrooge has shown us the purging, fiery heroic path. He embarked on the courageous descent to the depths of his grief and pain—his dark abyss. Scrooge is an archetype—an ideal model to emulate. So let's look at his adventure, albeit initially a journey of terror.

I am sure most of you remember what happened to ole Ebenezer Scrooge, whether you watched the movie or read the book, *A Christmas Carol* by Charles Dickens. The cantankerous Scrooge contaminated the Christmas spirit of his neighbors with his negative and hostile attitude. During the days, work and hoarding money consumed Scrooge, a bona fide workaholic and miser. He did not furnish his workers' pay raises. Nor did he offer money to the poor. In short, Scrooge was in *conflict* with the world around him. So the Ghost of Christmas Past—a metaphor for our nightmarish dreams, crises, and conflicts in our lives—visited Scrooge in order to light a fire under his ornery rump by revealing "his past." First, the ghost told Scrooge that the visitation was meant for his *welfare*. Next, the ghost gave Scrooge a vision of a lonely, little boy sitting in a chair and reading a book. Immediately, Scrooge recognized the boy as himself and sobbed. Scrooge probably experienced a lonely boyhood and felt deprived of nurture and love from his parents or caregivers. But this story marks a universal motif or symbol; this wounded child exists in all of us, and the child tends to create conflict within us and with others—nobody escapes the pain of life.

Soon, it became easier for Scrooge to weep, and his heart began to soften. The purge bestows many benefits. For example, we may grieve at the loss and death of a loved one, but in Scrooge's case, he needed to grieve, release, and bury the emotional wounds of childhood. In short, the *death* of the wounds of the past transpired, and a *rebirth* or *resurrection* toward human growth and potentiality was possible. Moreover, for Scrooge, the purge destroyed the false self-identity or social mask he had constructed over the years. He had identified himself as a rapacious businessman, tough and mean and a verbal bully. In short, Scrooge mistakenly believed the adaptive and learned social and cultural roles he had taken on composed his genuine self-identity. These masks or false identities were, truly, adaptive behaviors that he used, in part, to cover his fear of experiencing the emotional wounds of the past. In this, Scrooge and Rafael are similar.

After the revelation of Scrooge's childhood, he proclaimed, "Spirit … show me no more! Conduct me home. Why do you delight to torture me?" (Dickens 2009, 36).

Most of us resemble Scrooge, for the fear and pain of the past stresses us, and we will do anything to avoid it. Generally, our initial response is to flee and run home to the security and dependency of our parents or some other familiar or dependent object, person, place, or thing (e.g., alcohol or drugs).

Yet, when the second ghost, Christmas Present, arrived, Scrooge remarked, "I learnt a lesson which is working now. To-night, if you have aught [sic] to teach me, let me profit by it" (Dickens 2009, 42).

Now Scrooge becomes transformed before our eyes. Scrooge implicitly possessed the ability to experience the grief and pain of the past, although he insisted that he could not, and more importantly, he learned and benefited from it.

Prior to his quest Scrooge denied his pain and, thereby, projected or expressed his hidden or unconscious pain through his negative and critical behavior of other people. Often when we experience conflict with others, the cause lies in our or their unsolved wounds of the past because we overprotect the wounded child within by constructing rigid defenses such as anger, projection (blaming our problems on others), denial, excessive narcissism, and so forth. When we courageously face and purge our past, we reduce fear, and then we become free to experience our unique selves by *letting go* of false identities or social masks self-constructed over the years. Hence, we can experience the ability to love authentically and fully and to move forward in our human growth. Furthermore, we become freer from the past, since we neither deny it nor overreact behaviorally. Rather, we shout with Scrooge, "I will honour [sic] Christmas in my heart, and try to keep it all year. I will live in the Past, Present, and the Future" (Dickens 2009, 78).

The ghost, through appropriate *fear* and *terror*, opened up Scrooge's conscious mind to increase his awareness and growth and help him say yes to life. The ghost compares to a messenger in our dreams, whose presence speaks not of an evil monster but emerges as a visitant, who comes in a seemingly paradoxical and disguised form as a destroyer of the wounds of the past and as a creator to heal and beautify the self (see chapter 15, "Dream One"). We should learn to listen to our inner voice and dreams. The practice of solitude and the use of a dream journal can assist us in this quest for self-knowledge (see chapter 15). Jung (1985, 152) maintained, "The unconscious is not a demonical monster. ... It only becomes dangerous when our conscious attitude to it is hopelessly wrong. To the degree we repress it, its danger increases."

We must learn to face pain and grief, whether early in life or later—we can't escape it—for the Ghost of Christmas Past always lurks within us. As professor Joseph Campbell (in Free

1996) maintained, whatever we *push down* in our unconscious will eventually *come up*. Some scholars maintain that the dream visitant or Ghost of Christmas Past represents our potential self and/or the divinity within that yearns for manifestation (Campbell in Patillo and Manchi 1988).

So ole Scrooge is an archetypal model for one who embarks on the hero's descent to where the wounds and pain abide. Prior to the ghost's visit, Scrooge was the stereotypical rigid, macho weirdo who denied his emotions and pain and never shed a tear. But during his purge of grief and pain, Scrooge neither became some king or queen of drama by weeping hysterically as a staged event showing himself as a victim in order to get attention, nor did he try to compel others to join him in his grief and pain. On the contrary, Scrooge wept in solitude with a balance of soft sensitivity and courageous strength. The purge or rite of purification *humanized* and *beautified* Scrooge like the pruning of a tree. But most of us resemble Scrooge because the pain just damn hurts, and so we whine and complain to the heavens. To whine renders us human, but we should never relinquish the human quest. Scrooge exemplified for us that the jewels of life exist in our dark abyss.

Scrooge embarked on a solitary journey. And ultimately we must make the descent in solitude, although we may have a guide like a parent or counselor. The practice of solitude (see chapter 12, "A Sacred Place") is important because, in the silence of solitude, we can discover our identity and hidden potentialities. In the novel *Lonesome Dove* by Larry McMurtry (1986, 18), the maverick cowboy, Call, walked away from the group to be alone because "he had discovered early on that his instincts needed privacy in which to operate."

Like Scrooge, others have gone before us in the solitary journey—Moses, Odysseus, Jesus, Mohammed, and the Buddha, to name a few. Reading these heroes' stories shows us that we are not alone. As Professor Campbell (1973, 25) maintained, "The heroes of all time have gone before us; the labyrinth is thoroughly known; we have only to follow the thread of the hero-path. And where we had thought to find an abomination, we shall find a god; … where we had thought to travel outward, we shall come to the center of our existence; where we had thought to be alone, we shall be with all the world."

Key Points

- Frightful dream figures intend to make us aware of things we tend to deny and repress; consequently, the intensity of terror from a dream relates directly to the degree of our denial and repression. Therefore, dream figures use fear to awake and teach us to heal and grow.
- The emotional wounds of the past dwell in the unconscious. Nightmarish dreams symbolically provide us with an internal teacher who warns us if we are in denial of our authentic and potential self (see chapter 15, "Dream One"). Likewise, dreams provide guidance for us; through them we can become more aware of and purge our wounded past of anger and inferiorities so that we can move forward in our growth and freedom and discover our unrealized potentialities.
- A dream journal can aid us in discovering the messages from our unconscious (see chapter 15).
- The practice of solitude, such as in meditation, yoga or chi gung will help us listen to our instinctive inner voice as a guide, as well as maintain psychological and spiritual balance (see chapter 12).
- With a parent or counselor (see chapter 12, "A Sacred Place"), children and teens can grieve and purge the emotional wounds of the past. The purge provides an emotional cleansing and death of the past. Then we can experience a rebirth or resurrection to our potential self and future.

TEN

The Tragic Losses of Liza and John

I'm including the stories in this chapter so that parents and educators can become more aware of the symptoms, development, and possible causes of depression and suicidal ideation. I believe that we can interpret these afflictions as tumultuous wake-up calls from the unconscious and that we can use them to create movement and change in the lives of those who are suffering—as a means to helping them move toward the fulfillment of their unrealized potentiality. Additionally, I will provide suggestions to help caregivers enact suicide prevention measures.

In the spring of 2000, on a Sunday evening, I received a phone call from Mr. Chase, the principal of Cougarville School. I immediately experienced a sense of foreboding because unexpected phone calls often carry grim news. Mr. Chase, in a melancholic tone, conveyed that Liza, a fourteen-year-old student at Cougarville, had committed suicide. Shock rocked my being; I had never thought Liza would actually commit suicide, although she had a history of hospitalization for suicidal ideation. Ms. Morrison, her teacher, and I had analyzed Liza's suicidal episodes primarily as an attention-seeking device rather than as severe depression and despair. Liza exhibited herself as the model student. Furthermore, we observed that Liza did not display any symptoms of depression or suicidal risk.

Suicide always commands staff's utmost attention. Moreover, for twenty years no teen had ever committed suicide on my watch, so to speak. Liza had not committed this fatal act while in attendance at Cougarville. Three months prior, Liza's mother had her admitted to a psychiatric hospital. A few weeks later, after being discharged, Liza participated in a partial hospitalization program, where she attended school. Liza had attended PHP for the past two months while she lived at home. Clearly, during this time Liza must have deteriorated into a serious state of depression, despair, and hopelessness. Her death disturbed me immensely. I suffered from remorse, guilt, confusion, and anger.

Liza had been one of the most intelligent students to attend Cougarville. She did not fit the typical mold of the Cougarville student, not just because of her intelligence but because, at only age fourteen, Liza exhibited an elevated maturity. Moreover, we never had any difficulty managing Liza's behavior because she seemed to feel safe and secure and didn't seem to be experiencing peer or academic pressure. Ms. Morrison actively pursued transitioning Liza back into regular education classes. But Liza's problem behavior at home prevented her mother and the home school district from returning her to the regular school setting.

As a Cougarville student, Liza did something quite special and rare. She read books. The majority of students had learning disabilities, so the only books I would occasionally see students read included S. E. Hinton novels like *The Outsiders* or *Tex*. I remember that Liza read a more sophisticated book, *Angela's Ashes* by Frank McCourt, an autobiography about McCourt's upbringing under enormously adverse conditions of poverty in a large family with an alcoholic father in Brooklyn, New York, and Ireland. Yet McCourt worked diligently to overcome these obstacles through education and jobs, and eventually, at about age nineteen, he immigrated to the United States. After college graduation, McCourt became a successful high school teacher in New York City. I used this story with Liza as an analogy of how anyone can overcome family or academic difficulties.

Liza's death angered me because she held so much potential. Her truant officer revealed that forensic investigators had concluded that Liza had endeavored to stop the suicide and escape from the rope around her neck. Liza really did not want to die. The truant officer, Ms. Smith, made a perspicacious observation. "Liza just wanted the *pain* to go away."

These words inundated my thoughts, along with the bewilderment and horror that she had actually taken her life. Liza's death haunted me and plunged me into a philosophical quandary. Why had Liza taken her life? I felt guilty because, in a sense, I had missed the signs or the depth of her pain. I felt so confident about my knowledge and analysis of adolescents and psychology. Something seemed amiss.

Then some weeks later, the bizarre, nightmarish suicidal contagion began. A staff member at Cougarville, John, committed suicide in a most horrific method: He cut the gas lines in his home, and to insure his death, he slashed his wrists and arms. Then, he lay in bed until the explosion occurred. Indeed, the house exploded and even damaged neighbors' homes. But, to John's utter horror, he survived with 80 percent of his body burned. He remained conscious enough to communicate by squeezing the hand of his fiancée; he lived about eight days before he died. Why would John take his life? His life seemed full. He had a teenage daughter and a fiancée. Evidently John, like Liza, had his *pain of life*, and he too wanted his pain to go away. Yet what could be so painful that he would leave his fiancée and daughter behind? The utter bizarreness and tragic irony included that John was the school psychologist.

Suicide can ignite a spree of suicides—a sociological and psychological contagion. Now with this second suicide, I wallowed in internal emotional turmoil. Confusion and panic rocked me because I harbored a deep secret. I too was suicidal, and I thought of the horrific possibility that I could be next. For months, suicidal ideation afflicted my mind. Anxiety and depression attacked me relentlessly, and I reeled in a psychological and spiritual crisis because my philosophical foundation of *love and work* had failed Liza and John, and now it was failing me. What was wrong with me?

My self-confidence shattered into oblivion, and the constant threat of further anxiety attacks, sleepless nights, and nightmares created havoc upon my psychological well-being. I kept wondering how much more could I take.

The Last Call: The Assault of the Unconscious and a New Dawn

My anxiety and depression began with an onslaught of nightmarish dreams in February 2000. I had maintained a dream journal for the past few years, and I had grown in my understanding of my own dream world to the point that I could often interpret my dreams as I awoke. But now the dreams evoked terror, bizarreness, and mass confusion. My mind blocked interpretation because the dreams induced such poignant anxiety and incongruence that, when I simply reviewed a dream, my emotions and psyche reexperienced the onslaught of psychic disturbance of the dream itself. Moreover, anxiety attacks assaulted me so frequently that I often had to take long walks. Anxiety attacks give one the terrible feeling of loss of control of the mind and emotions and the fear of ensuing madness. My usual coping mechanisms of reading, meditating, walking, exercising, working, and socializing with friends and family waned in effectiveness.

Now I felt trapped in a quandary. Months before, my confidence in my life and work had boomed, but suddenly I had plunged into the abyss of depression and worthlessness. I felt imprisoned in the despair and hopelessness that had led to Liza and John's suicides. The constant threat and terror of further anxiety attacks and depression produced hopelessness. I feared to sleep at night because anxiety would assault me as soon as I lay in bed. I dreaded being terrorized further by dreams. Then periodically, a wave of boredom and sadness would trigger a sense of isolation, depression, and alienation, which would further deplete my self-confidence, esteem, and masculinity into self-reproach and self-hate. I fantasized about destroying myself with an AK-47 and annihilating every aspect of my physical, psychological, and spiritual being. I imagined that bliss and peace could only be experienced via self-annihilation into pure nothingness. One day as I walked through a remote park and wept, my prayers turned into a harangue and fury at the transcendent one. I was furious that my life had suddenly become meaningless and void; it seemed unjust.

During this time, I just endeavored to persevere and not get into that deep despair where suicide lurks in the foreground as a viable option. I visited family and friends because I knew that isolation marks the red zone for suicide. I am a private person, so talking about my crisis and depression and anxiety with anyone was difficult. I felt shame. I was a grown man at age forty-seven and a psychotherapist to boot and I could not master my own psyche and emotions. I felt my manhood being tortuously emasculated.

Of course, I can hear you shouting at me right now, "Hey Bentley, why didn't you go see a psychotherapist yourself!" You are correct, but a problem existed—I had already done that. In 1982, I reacted to depression because of job stress with a past pattern from my late adolescence. I relapsed into cocaine use that fueled more depression. So I participated in psychotherapy for a few years, which was an indispensable experience. I worked assiduously, exploring the depths of my childhood, adolescence, family, relationships, and internal psyche. As Jung (1989, 58) summed, "Psychoanalysis demands a sacrifice which no other science demands of its adherents: ruthless self-knowledge." How could I work as a psychotherapist anyhow if I did not examine my psyche and do my internal work? Maybe I am just stubborn, but I decided not to return to psychotherapy unless no other option existed. I thought that to go back into therapy was to place myself in a *dependent* psychological position. I needed to look hard at my life, and I thought the anxiety and depression meant something bigger—something different—that I needed to figure out.

During the horrific spring of 2000, I needed to talk with someone. Three people made suggestions to me that would help bring clarity to my experience and would plant seeds for a plan of action. First, I knew of one person I could comfortably talk to—my friend Jake, the former director at Cougarville. He had obtained a new job as an assistant superintendent in a Chicago suburban school district. Jake, a psychologist, would soon earn a PhD in education. We'd performed as a solid team at Cougarville, and we thought alike about adolescent psychology and treatment. Jake is an intelligent, practical, and compassionate man. In mid-April, I needed direct and honest feedback on my plight, and I knew Jake would provide it, so I visited him at his home. After I described my depression and anxiety, Jake pointed out the importance of goals and that I had probably stagnated in my professional growth. He advised teaching psychology at a junior college. I had thought about that option, but I mentioned my dream of writing a book on adolescence, and we chatted for a while. Then Jake spoke directly and poignantly. He pointed out that, often at Cougarville, it seemed fair for me to joke with a student and put my hand on the student's shoulder, but God forbid if I would allow the youth to return the same human gesture. Then Jake deftly stressed that J. D. Salinger was Holden Caulfield, and he had written a fantastic book because it stemmed from his own experience. Jake hit me hard on my *shadow*, and he provided an effective direct blow that compelled me to look deeper at myself and my defensive, self-protective, and guarded behaviors. In short, if I sought to write a good book, I would need to explore and share more of my experiences, shadows, and pitfalls.

In early May 2000, I attended the Debs-Thomas-Harrington Dinner at the Congress Hotel in downtown Chicago. The dinner kicks off an annual awards and fund-raising event for progressive union leaders, politicians, and activists. In a large hall with three hundred attendees, I sat at a circular dining table with about ten people as we waited for dinner to be served. I did not know most of the people, so naturally I struck up a conversation to discover what interesting things people did with their lives. I began to converse with a woman named Carol, an elegant and attractive woman around age sixty, and I inquired what she did professionally. Carol explained that she worked as a teacher and writer. She had published a book on breast cancer that centered on the unity of health with the green ecology movement. I responded that I harbored a dream of writing a book for adolescents someday. She queried curiously about my profession. I reported to her my work at Cougarville with the likes of the infamous Charles the Beast. Immediately she gave me an unforgettable expression. With effusive compassion, she commanded, "You must write!" Carol explained the importance of journal writing for forty-five minutes or three pages a day. She advised me to write whatever comes to my mind and preferably in the morning, since the unconscious remains active during that time of day.

The next day, I embraced journal writing in earnest. I will never forget Carol. Writing helped me not just to express my emotional depths, but it seemed to lessen the anxiety attacks and bouts of depression. Thus, there seemed to be an implicit connection between writing and my anxiety attacks, fears, depression, and suicidal ideation.

A week later, I consulted with a friend, Ann. After I mentioned the horrific anxiety attacks and depression, she stressed something that I will never forget. "You are being assaulted by your unconscious— don't analyze it, just let it happen. It's like a throwing-up process. Exercising, laughing, and crying will help move your psyche forward." Ann's words brought huge relief and instilled in me a different way of viewing the unconscious. Now I viewed my conscious ego-self not as weak and worthless. Rather, the unconscious called me forth "to duty" and to write the book of my dreams on adolescence. Jung conceived that normal persons possess the same complexes as neurotics, and he stressed that psychotherapy should not get caught up in mother and father complexes because everyone has them. Jung (1989, 182) maintained that the central question we should pose is this: "What is the task which the patient does not want to fulfil [sic]? What difficulty is he trying to avoid?" For me, I repressed my dream to write, yet ironically, in writing rested the means to enhance my growth, individuation, and independence.

Yet due to my self-doubt and resistance, I had fallen back into what Campbell (1999, 213–14, 255) conceptualized as the *Waste Land*, which comes from living an inauthentic life. In living an authentic life, the individual follows the societal script—what you're supposed to do (in other words, overidentifying with your social role or *persona*)—but does not follow his or her heart, or the "spontaneity of your noble nature." I sense the waste land experience is common for many adults, particularly during midlife (roughly age forty to fifty-five) when, suddenly, a marriage, with grown children, has soured and needs a sense of renewal and direction. But sometimes that fails, and the marriage ends in a divorce; or the individual finds his or her career stagnant and no longer able to provide a sense of satisfaction. Additionally, people might feel an inner emptiness that really yearns for some unrealized fulfillment. However, the fear of change can spark such anxiety, self-doubt, and melancholy that the individual would rather remain in the status quo.

So my nightmares likened to what Campbell called *the call of the hero/heroine*. Similarly, the biblical Jonah did not initially adhere to God's call, and consequently, he was swallowed into the belly of a whale. I too had been submerged in horrific, dark unconscious forces because I had repressed the messages from my dreams. Campbell compares *the call* using the quest for the Holy Grail. This quest, he maintains, prevails as the solution for being lost in the waste land. Campbell (1999, 212) summarized, "This is a wonderful story: that which we intend, that which is the journey, that which is the goal, is the fulfillment of something that never was on earth before— namely, your own potentiality."

Jung wrote that humans have a "personal unconscious" that contains the memories of our past experiences, our losses, our attitudes, our neuroses or complexes, and so forth. However, there exists also a "collective unconscious" of universal, inherited instinctive images, motifs, or themes that Jung called archetypes, such as "the call," whether the *first call* of adolescence or the *call* of midlife, to duty in order to discover our inner human *potentialities*. So, like the recalcitrant Scrooge, I too received a visitant to awaken me. My unconscious called me to change, to duty, and to discover my unrealized potentialities. In other words, internally, I needed to discover something more within me, and externally, I had to learn something more about the adventure of life. For example, I needed to take the initiative, make the commitment, and challenge myself to fulfill my dream of writing a book on adolescence. In addition, I wanted to broaden my experience by living abroad, touring more countries, and learning about more cultures. In short, I experienced that instinctive feeling or intuition that strikes on occasion, saying, *There must be something more to life than what I am presently experiencing. What is it? I want to find it so that I won't have any regrets in life.*

The Parallels of Adolescence and Midlife

Eventually, my experience of the unconscious assault led to deep realizations about me and adolescence. In a sense, the crisis evoked a recapitulation of my adolescent life. The relentless flood of powerful emotions, such as anxiety and fear, compared to the surge of emotions during midadolescence—the great barrier (see chapter 1). In the same vein, the anxiety and fear, along with my thoughts of self-hate and self-aggression, related directly to the triadic scourge of inferiority (see chapter 8). The crisis and melancholy sparked feelings of uncertainty about my identity and social role. Finally, I had to face the dependency issue of being trapped in a job that had reached its apex for my learning and growth. But like many adolescents, I resisted and feared change. However, albeit paradoxically, the horrific assault became a harbinger for a death and rebirth in my life that moved me toward a new dawn.

The parallels between adolescence and midlife are as follows:

1. Adolescence marks the *first call* to give way to the death of childhood dependency and experience a rebirth toward adulthood. During this death and rebirth, adolescents discover their identities and social roles in the world. Midlife marks the apparent *last call*—to let go or give way to the death of the structures (e.g., job, social role, and self-image) constructed over the years that now have become an obstruction to one's personal growth and to one's unfulfilled goals, dreams, and potentiality.

2. In adolescence, females and males experience a biological birth as sexual beings capable of procreation (menstruation and male sexual potency). At midlife, adults experience the waning of youth and biological procreative potency (menopause and impotency).

3. Adolescence consists as the separation and loss of childhood. In midlife, adults experience the separation and loss of their youthful manhood or womanhood. For males, during their youthful manhood, they generally used their aggressive instinct as a source of social identity and power, whether in athletics or a job. In contrast, females, during their youthful womanhood, tend to use their sexuality as a source of social identity and power. At midlife, the biological shift compels adults to change and adapt. Campbell used a light bulb as a metaphor and said that, at midlife, adults should not identify with the body (the glass bulb) because it is dying, but rather adults should identify with the inner spirit (the light) (Campbell in Patillo and Manchi 1998).

Author's Suggestions on a Family's Loss from Suicide and Prevention

The suicide of a family member is one of the most poignant and tragic experiences anyone can encounter. Yet, suicide is, unfortunately, a reality. However, if such a tragedy hits a family, the remaining family members should make a plan of action for coping with the problem. Five coping mechanisms include: (1) incorporating symbolic burial rites into the grieving process, (2) getting professional assistance if deemed necessary, (3) using journal writing, (4) reading memoirs with the theme of *triumph over adversity*, and (5) getting involved in volunteer work.

1. Part of the grieving process should be symbolic burial rites. Parents can use their imagination and judgment to determine what symbols or possessions of their child would be most beneficial for the family to communicate a sense of acknowledgment, release, and farewell at the funeral or gravesite. I suggest that parents think of grieving as a one-year process. During this period, the family will move through the difficult passage of key holidays, the deceased's birthday, and the anniversary of his or her death.

2. If deemed necessary, a few sessions with a psychotherapist or trained minster could bring an independent voice and perspective to this extraordinarily stressful period. An experienced third party can open channels of communication among family members to assist them in the grieving process when dealing with complicated emotions such as sorrow, loss, anger, guilt, or resentment and, thereby, open a way for the family to me toward resolution of this crisis so all of the family members can move forward.

3. Journal writing is an excellent way to express emotions of grief, loss, anger, guilt, and so forth. It allows the writer to express whatever she desires without fear of offending anyone. And if she so chooses, she can simply rip up the written paper and put it in the garbage as a symbolic gesture of release. If these emotions are not released appropriately, then the unexpressed feelings can become toxic in the mind-body, resulting in bouts of lethargy, melancholy, and resentment. Therefore, writing can provide a psychological and emotional release as well as perspective (see chapter 16). In a similar vein, remember my friend Ann's recommendation to me; crying, laughing, and exercising help move one's psyche forward.

4. Reading memoirs of triumph over adversity is a valuable resource. Through these tales, we access an empathetic and independent voice in order to avoid a sense of hopelessness, isolation, or resentment. Books like *Lucky* by Alice Sebold, who wrote eloquently and beautifully of her poignant endeavor to overcome sexual assault provide this voice. *The Glass Castle* by Jeannette Walls, who wrote with humor of her disturbing upbringing of poverty, hunger, and parental neglect as her vagabond family wandered aimlessly across the United States is another example. In the end, Jeannette and her sister eventually triumphed over their chaotic life by attending Columbia University. Psychologist Viktor Frankl wrote a poignant account of his victory over his gruesome Holocaust experience in the excellent book *Man's Search for Meaning*. There are also memoirs by parents whose child had died from suicide.

5. Research (Goleman 1996, 84) has shown that volunteer work, such as working in a soup kitchen, tutoring, or coaching a sport, provides a means to alter one's moods away from melancholy or depression. This external activity creates "movement" away from the human tendency to become self-absorbed after a trauma or in depression.

Suicide Prevention

I would like to emphasize four areas of suicide prevention. These include: (1) awareness of the symptoms of depression and suicidal risk; (2) direct communication; (3) an emphasis on exercising, laughing, and crying for emotional and psychological movement; and (4) for individuals who show symptoms of depression and are considered at-risk with suicide ideation, reading this chapter and chapters 16 and 17.

1. The typical symptoms for depression and behaviors that imply suicidal risk include, among others, emotional withdrawal, a sense of hopelessness, anxiety and sleep problems, nightmares, decline in academic progress, lethargy, isolation, and inability to laugh at something clearly funny. Often we can experience stressful periods in life, but we usually adjust after a few days. When, for a teenager, these moods and behaviors extend beyond a week, this is a red flag calling for a plan of action. Also, look for possible social factors, such as a breakup of a romantic relationship or a suicide in the community, or reckless behaviors, such as driving a car at excessive speeds or climbing dangerous cliffs. Finally, listen carefully to what your child says, paying attention to "hints" or innuendos about suicide. Often those with serious depression and suicidal risks give a final verbal message of their intention to commit suicide—a plea for help—to someone who is emotionally close to them.

2. The next step is to focus on direct communication. First, validating our perception of a situation with other competent individuals is valuable because sometimes we could be wrong. If parents agree about a concern, they might broaden their perspective by talking with teachers or any other persons in contact with your child, such as coaches or arts instructors. This will help them determine whether others have noticed the same signs—withdrawal, melancholy, decline in mental concentration, and so forth—in their child. Second, I suggest that parents talk directly with their child—a most difficult task. However, doing so is much better than the regret and guilt that will come if we've neglected to take this important step. Of course, the purpose of this discussion is not to play the role of a psychotherapist but to determine whether your perception is accurate and

to ease your emotional concern. A way to broach this difficult subject would be to again discuss and review the general aspects of adolescent psychology from chapter 1. Tell the child that, during adolescence and throughout life in general, we experience separations and changes that might spark a sense of loss and melancholy and might feel like a death. Explain that everyone must courageously move forward and experience a rebirth of sorts into adulthood, new relationships, and new challenges like college or a job. Use your judgment as to the best time and place to talk. The important aspect is how we talk about depression and suicide. A casual way to open communication is to take a walk or drive together, which eases conversation. Walking provides a form of exercise that helps move your child out of a stuck emotional state. Be sure to use the "I message" technique recommended in chapter 1. For example, you might say, "Son, I am reviewing the changes of adolescence now because when you speak so little for over a week now, I feel that you might have some things on your mind because you look like you are feeling a bit down. Is anything eating at you deep inside?"

During my experience with depression, I realized that *depressed* means feeling down, so the simple solution rests in the antithesis; I had to get up and create *movement* in my life (see chapters 16 and 17). And this movement entails two aspects. First, suicide ideation signals a warning and symbolically means that something in one's life needs to die or change, such as the pain from past relationships, whether a marital divorce or a romance; personal failure; sexual or physical abuse; or loss and abandonment of parents or others. I deeply sense that, usually, the crux of the issue of suicidal ideation lies in the source of one's pain of life. Often, this pain relates to the shadow of inferiority that suddenly has overrun the individual, resulting in self-reproach and the self-hate (see chapters 8, 16, and 17). Second, related to this phenomenon of the death of something rests the necessity for action, such as with the soldier's arduous task to separate from their social role, duty, and behavior as a combatant. The individual must grieve, purge, and *let go* of something from the past. And he or she must take action to create change and move his or her life in a new direction, perhaps toward an unrealized dream or goal—a resurrection (see chapters 5, 16, and 17). In your conversation you can be a sounding board for your teenager. In other words, you can practice reflective listening, so the teen can consider various aspects of his or her life that might be the cause of emotional pain. And you can explore your child's future goals or plans.

So with this feeling about death comes the solution—the necessity of taking action through some form of change or resurrection. I want to stress the importance of using the subject matter of *death and resurrection* because, if your child has suicidal ideation, this language affirms empathically their inner experience and can bridge your communication—we should not deny the idea of death. Even if your child denies feeling depressed, you can provide the general information that depression means that we must create movement toward change in our lives, which can provide the necessary, vital element of hope. Therefore, this discussion on death, change, and resurrection acknowledges to the teen a sense of congruence and attunement with his or her inner emotional world and, possibly, compels the teen to think about his or her unique and ultimate human responsibility—as Campbell notes, to seek and find his or her human potentiality. Furthermore, this frank acknowledgment of death can eliminate any fantasies or false notions of suicide as a romantic and viable final exit.

If your child remains reticent and clearly does not want to open up to you, then you can suggest that he or she talk with an independent party, perhaps a psychotherapist, to work through this difficult period. (See chapter 12 for suggestions on finding a psychotherapist.)

3. As my friend so aptly put it, "Exercising, laughing, and crying help move one's psyche." This maxim aids in the assessment for symptoms of depression as well as a solution. For example, parents could watch a movie with their teen, either a comedy or a tragic drama. If your child shows little emotional response, that would provide a possible affirmation of melancholy. Meanwhile, the tragic drama (a tearjerker) and comedy provides a means for crying and laughing, which can help move the youth out of a stuck, melancholic emotional state. When someone has difficulty laughing, it seems clear that something is not right. A movie about suicide, such as the *Dead Poets Society* or *The Virgin Suicides* (also a book), can provide a means to broach and talk about this poignant subject. A psychotherapist with whom I worked would tell his adolescent clients with suicidal ideation, "It's okay to think about suicide, but it is not okay to do it." Again this statement is an affirmation of the child's emotional state. Yet it also creates boundaries and an ethical value and responsibility for one's life. Through activities like films and walking that allow the teen to cry, laugh, and exercise, you can help create psychological and emotional release and objectivity as a strategy for breaking through this emotional crisis.

4. Lastly, I live in the Philippines, where my friend Mary read and edited an earlier draft of this chapter and chapters 16 and 17. Mary had decided to give these chapters to a friend of hers to read because this female friend was suicidal. I did not mind that Mary took the

liberty because a core purpose of these chapters is to aid those at suicidal risk. Mary's friend, Jane, age twenty-five, is college educated and employed in a professional position. She experienced depression and despair about being trapped in a long-term romantic relationship that had turned sour—metaphorically, it was dying. Mary's conversations with her friend weighed heavy on Mary emotionally because Jane spoke openly of suicide as a viable option for her life. After reading the chapters, Jane told Mary, "I think that I need to take a hard look at my life." Now this statement generated *movement* toward inner self-analysis, self-realization, and possible change. Weeks later, Jane left the Philippines to stay with relatives in another country. All I know is that Jane created movement in her life—change—and she is alive. In a sense, her actions encompassed a death (separation from a relationship that had died) and a rebirth or resurrection to a new situation in a different country—not as an act of escape or isolation, but with a plan of action with the emotional support and stability of family relatives. Her actions encapsulate my intention for these chapters to be read by someone entangled in this type of personal crisis. Therefore, if a parent has concerns about depression and suicidal ideation with their child, I suggest that they consider whether they would like to have their teen read all or parts of chapters 10, 16, and 17).

Key Points

- Nightmares can often act as precursors and messengers about unconscious problems and psychic imbalance that need our attention.
- Often our neuroses, like melancholy, reflect immobility and an avoidance of something. We usually avoid something from our past or present that obstructs

our need for personal growth, individuation, and independence.

- The *Waste Land* represents living an inauthentic life; often this occurs when one gets trapped in his or her social role such as a job that fails to provide a sense of life purpose and fulfillment. Emancipation from the waste land comes from listening to one's instinctive inner voice—one's heart—as a guide for fulfillment.

- Personal crises are messages from the unconscious to awaken us from a stagnant, unfulfilled life and to move us forward to discover our unique potentiality.

- The parallels between adolescence and midlife consist of similar socio-emotional and psychological issues, such as separation and change, dependency versus independence, and facing new frontiers in the development of one's unique identity and sexuality.

- When families are coping with a loss from suicide, they can (1) ensure that the grieving process includes symbolic burial rites, (2) seek professional assistance if deemed necessary, (3) use journal writing, (4) read memoirs with the theme of *triumph over adversity*, and (5) participate in volunteer work.

- The author suggests four strategies for the prevention of suicide. These include: (1) awareness of the symptoms of depression and suicidal risk; (2) direct communication; (3) an emphasis on exercising, laughing, and crying for emotional and psychological movement; and (4) reading memoirs of authors' experience with depression and suicide ideation, such as those found in this chapter and in chapters 16 and 17.

PART THREE

Internal Revolution

The purpose of part 3 is to define and expand upon the Atlanta politician Michael Lomax's suggestion for the necessity of an internal revolution (see chapter 8). In short, an internal revolution stands for self-change and means the strengthening of one's individuality through increased self-awareness and self-knowledge. An internal revolution embodies the difficult task of facing one's shadows, inferiorities, and pain of life in a way that can bring greater understanding, healing, and freedom from one's emotional anxieties and fears, anger and melancholy, and emotional dependency.

Self-change can be hard work, but it provides a deep sense of personal fulfillment. I have spent many years in this effort. After my personal crisis of depression and suicidal ideation, I realized that I had to explore more deeply into my unconscious for greater self-understanding. For the past eleven years, I have had the conscious intention of finding *shortcuts* toward self-change—not only for myself, but also for the common adult or teen in order to make the path more understandable, accessible, and easier to navigate. Relying on many years of reading, research, experimentation, and experience, I have presented in parts 3 and 4 what I learned in terms of the most effective "shortcuts" toward self-knowledge and personal growth. In part 3, four activities or techniques target specific aspects of our human nature in order to develop a solid foundation upon which the individual can create his or her own autonomous psychological-emotional-spiritual boot camp of sorts. These include reading (the intellect), solitude in a sacred place (the spiritual), recapitulation (the emotional), and awareness of the death instinct (mind-body). Through willful intention and consistent effort, these activities and techniques will aid one in establishing an internal fortress for self-power, self-healing, personal growth, and increased emotional intelligence.

I will present suggestions on how a parent can begin to incorporate for their child the practice and skill of reading, solitude, and an increased awareness of self-sabotaging behaviors (the death instinct). Meanwhile, educators can creatively think of ways to use the chapters on reading and the death instinct (self-sabotaging behaviors) in the classroom. I believe that these behaviors and instinct are a major catalyst toward interpersonal conflict (see chapter 5), academic failure, school dropouts, incarceration, suicide (see chapter 10), and so forth. Therefore parents, educators, and teens need to be aware of and understand this powerful human instinct and learn how to harness its positive potentiality. Recapitulation, a technique to release one's emotional baggage of the past, is meant for adults but could be optional for a teen with parental consent.

ELEVEN

Internal Revolution Tactic 1: The Power of the Word—Reading

The internal revolution that Atlanta politician Michael Lomax proposes (see chapter 8) epitomizes exactly what black youth like Marcus need. Such a revolution is likely something nearly everyone needs. An internal revolution provides an offensive strategy by which we can gain self-knowledge in the psychological war against anxiety, fear, emotional wounds, and a self-destructive force inside us that can trigger aggression and self-destruction. The nuts and bolts for this internal revolution relate to partaking in three activities or techniques that will develop and strengthen one's intellectual, spiritual, and emotional character, respectively. First, intellectually, I'm specifically referring to reading. A child should learn to read between the ages of six and twelve. However, if parents discover that their child reads significantly below his or her grade level, they can always request a special education evaluation to determine if the child has a learning disability. An excellent website, "Reading rockets," offers reading tips for parents and educators. The site is located at http://www.readingrockets.org/.

The second activity is the inward path of spiritual solitude to seek self-knowledge (see chapter 12). And the third is the use of a technique called *recapitulation* that provides a means to eject the emotional baggage of false beliefs of inferiority or self-hate within (see chapter 13).

This chapter aims to reinforce for parents and educators that reading books is a powerful means of finding self-illumination and initiating self-change. I will present examples of the power of reading through the lives of three twentieth-century individuals and my own, showing how reading provides an essential intellectual foundation for continued growth in one's intellectual, emotional, and spiritual development. Meanwhile, educators might be able to use the enclosed material creatively in the classroom, particularly with minority students or those who tend to belittle the value of education.

Lomax stressed the necessity of the *inward* path, and as mentioned in chapter 1, the essential task of adolescence is taking this inward journey to discover one's unique identity, which ultimately transcends color or race. The black revolutionary Malcolm X experienced this exact epiphany when he traveled to Mecca, Saudi Arabia, and was astonished to meet "blue eyed blond" Muslims (Malcolm X 1973, 362). This encounter changed Malcolm X's philosophical foundation from being racially exclusive to racially inclusive—a huge illumination that further evolved his self-transformation. So how does one experience a "transformation" or "internal revolution" like Malcolm X or as Lomax proposes? The literature (Campbell in Patillo and Manchi 1988) informs us that only two paths exist. The first moves us through *trials and tribulations*, as demonstrated by figures like Odysseus, Job, Scrooge, or Malcolm X, who became transformed by their difficult and painful ordeals, such as war, sickness, disease, unconsciousness assaults from dreams, prison, and so forth. The second path consists of a *transformation of consciousness*— the experience when our self-perception or awareness of the world changes, as Malcolm X encountered. Therefore, Malcolm X models for us this *inward* transformation of consciousness. This chapter will show how reading books and getting an education transformed him as well.

Reading: A Means to Enlightenment

Literacy skills in reading and writing supply a necessary educational foundation before we go inward. Language is a humanizing force because it formulates our ability to identify thoughts and emotions, to communicate with others, and to increase knowledge and offers a means by which we can cross the invisible threshold of the spiritual— for in the beginning was the Word, and the Word was God.

No one better exemplifies the power of words, language, or reading than author Richard Wright. He wrote of his upbringing in the Jim Crowe South with an impoverished childhood of hunger, physical abuse, parental alcoholism, and desertion. Due to negative adult role models, Wright became a drunkard as a child at age six and killed a kitten—a warning of a violent potentiality. But Wright channeled (in other words, sublimated) this potential destructive energy into learning, reading, and writing. For words, books and knowledge revealed a path to freedom and transformation for him: "Even a Negro, entrapped by ignorance and exploitation—as I had been—could, if he had the will and the love for it, learn to read and understand the world in which he lived" (1993a, 436)

Human rational thought and language compose the basis for civilized and enriched cultures. Moreover, language helps us to identify and understand the messages from our unconscious minds. Words and language sustain us, allowing us not just to write or read books to obtain knowledge, but also to identify internal emotions and to interact energetically in the world. As Wright (1993a, 294– 95) wrote, "I hungered for books, new ways of looking and seeing. … Reading grew into a passion. … Reading was like a drug, a dope. The novels created moods in which I lived for days. … It was nothing less than a sense of life itself."

We need mentors who influence us positively. Wright questioned Ella, a school teacher, about a book she read—*Bluebeard and His Seven Wives* by Anatole France. While she described the story of Bluebeard, Richard experienced the power of the word and story. He wrote, "The tale made the world around me be, throb, live. …

Reality changed, the look of things altered, and the world became peopled with magical presences" (Wright 1993a, 45).

Wright's experience exemplifies one of the most effective activities by which a parent can instill in his or her child the interest in and skill of reading—simply reading stories, bedtime stories, for example, to their child at an early age. You can start doing this when the child is around age three and can talk and cognitively follow a simple story. This will open the world of the child's creative imagination, as it did for Wright, an essential development for the brain and cognitive processes. The smartest people I know were all avid readers in their childhood.

Deceased authors can also be mentors, teachers, and guides for us. At age twenty-two, I decided to change my life. I had become entrapped in dependency on alcohol and drugs. I returned to college, and within weeks, a book illuminated my soul—the Greek classic *The Odyssey* by Homer, wherein the hero, Odysseus, synthesized two seemingly contradictory opposites, love and aggression. On the one hand, Odysseus engaged the world as an inquirer and lover of humanity; however, if necessary, he became a cunning and tenacious warrior. Thus, Odysseus modeled a balanced and strengthened manhood for me.

Books, words, and education transformed Malcolm X. He served seven years in the dark abyss of prison where, through a mentor and education, he experienced a land of light:

> The first man I met in prison who made any positive impression on me whatever was a fellow inmate, "Bimbi …" the first Negro convict I'd known who didn't respond to "What'cha know, Daddy?" … What fascinated me with him most of all was that he was the first man I had ever seen command total respect … with his words. … He told me I should take advantage of the prison correspondence courses and the library. … Where else but in a prison could I have attacked my ignorance by being able to study intensely sometimes as much as fifteen hours a day? (Malcolm X 1973, 153, 154, 180)

The teacher and writer Frank McCourt (1997, 259) grew up in abject poverty in Ireland, yet his teacher boomed, "Your mind is your house and if you fill it with rubbish from the cinemas it will rot in your head. You might be poor, your shoes might be broken, but your mind is a palace." Reading and education furnished a means of profound enlightenment for Wright, Malcolm X, McCourt, and me; they brought to us Maslow's *peak experiences* (see chapter 3). Finally, education also emancipated Wright, Malcolm X, and McCourt from the chains and abyss of poverty and prison.

After a foundation of education mastery, one can begin the inward path along which invisible demons, dragons, or monsters must be faced and extinguished (see chapters 12 and 13). If we harbor a dream—whether that dream is to be a doctor, a scientist, an engineer, or the president; to eject the false self-images of inferiority; or to face inner sorrow—but we then say to ourselves, "Oh, I couldn't do that," professor Joseph Campbell (in Patillo and Manchi 1988) counseled, "Then 'that' is your dragon." Ironically, our repressed dream becomes our dragon or monster. The unconscious holds an extraordinary power inside us that yearns and seeks the manifestation of our potentiality—the undiscovered self within. So reading supplies a necessary preparatory skill—like going through military training—prior to the inward descent toward an internal revolution.

Key Points

- An internal revolution provides a necessary offensive strategy for facing the internal psychological war against anxiety, fear, emotional wounds, and a self-destructive force inside us that can trigger aggression and self-destruction.
- The first activity or technique necessary for an internal revolution is mastery of reading and writing. Reading books is a powerful resource for self-illumination (*peak experiences*) and self-change and an essential intellectual

foundation for continued growth in one's intellectual, emotional, and spiritual development.

- The path toward self-change is twofold. We must first move through trials and tribulations. Then we can achieve a transformation of consciousness, perceiving ourselves and the world anew.
- Reading to a child starting from a very early age opens the world of the child's creative imagination, an essential part of the development of the brain and cognitive processes.

Twelve

Internal Revolution Tactic 2: A Sacred Place

Daily, we encounter the stresses of life, such as school, work, illness, relationships and family, news of terror and death, and economic concerns. Professor Joseph Campbell counseled that, in order for us to free ourselves from these concerns, we must have a *sacred place*. A sacred place can be anywhere that brings you comfort. Reading a book in a quiet room, sitting in a place of worship, lighting a candle and sitting, listening to soft music, and walking in nature are just a few of the many possibilities. A sacred place allows an adult or a teen to get *centered* and shut out the demands of the world and to sit in "solo"—solitude. To begin with, being in the sacred place for one to five minutes a day builds a foundation, and eventually you could increase your sacred place time to twenty minutes. Morning is the best time to do this, but anytime will do; consistency will render fulfillment. Solitude marks a time to reflect about your dreams, goals, career, God, and spirituality and to let go of your social role, whether as a student, teacher, business owner, or any of the myriad other social identities which we may identify. Jung (1976, 105) called this social mask the *persona*, but we shouldn't *overidentify* with our persona because it veils our authentic self. Your *intention* reigns indispensable; the unconscious will honor your intention to discover your hidden human potentialities, goals, and dreams.

If you start spending time in your sacred place, subtle changes will begin to happen. For example, you'll experience an increased awareness of the self, of people, and of the environment; your thoughts and emotions will become more balanced; and you will notice that your concentration has enhanced and your fear has decreased. Eventually you will experience a sense of the presence and support of invisible hands. A Zen poem by Zenrin Kushu reads, "Sitting quietly, doing nothing, spring comes, the grass grows by itself" (quoted in Watts 1989, 134).

In solitude your deeper self will slowly surface, and in the meantime, your dormant internal potentialities await discovery. Jung called this the "undiscovered self." To know oneself, one must spend time with oneself. Solitude will increase your self-knowledge—true power. *The Upanishads* (Prabhavanada and Manchester 1971, 51–52), a sacred text from India, maintained that, "He who knows that immutable Self … knows all things, and realizes the Self in all."

As noted in chapter 1, the key internal force or guide necessary for an internal revolution consists of learning to listen to your inner voice—your gut feeling—of *instinct*, which the writer Campbell conceived as the *wisdom of the body*. It appears that instinct serves as a bridge for our conscious mechanism to obtain guidance from the unconscious, especially in stressful or dangerous situations. Nietzsche wrote that instinct and reason operate in accord as guides toward the good—toward God. Our deep inner voice—instinct—functions like an internal magical wand or summoning charm, which guides us toward self-knowledge and in our external actions. Jung (1991, 184) defined the inner voice as, "the voice of a fuller life, of a wider, more comprehensive consciousness."

A sacred place compares to a dojo where a martial artist trains, but here you master the art of self-knowledge and, thereby, develop profound psychological understanding of the dark, unconscious underworld so you can protect yourself. The art of self-knowledge compares to a martial art technique to nonviolently disarm a threat or to employing a mental laser beam or casting a magic spell to melt away the illusory masks that people wear for false power and control. In short, in a sacred place you can learn to arm yourself with and to master the necessary psychological weaponry (trust of your instincts and emotions and intuitive awareness of human motives and the dynamism of the unconscious) so you can combat life assertively, but nonviolently, without the fear of passive impotence. And by doing so, you will maintain a strong femininity or masculinity. In *The Art of War*, Sun Tzu (1971, 77) counseled, "To subdue the enemy without fighting is the acme of skill."

Bringing light to the dark forces of the unconscious feels like creating magic because you will see the world differently, with increased clarity, valor, fearlessness, and power. The true dark art consists of mastering the self and the dark unknown unconscious, where the treasures and potentialities of light await discovery. Through this discovery, a feeling of self-mastery will prevail. Your thought will be in accord with your instinct, a compassion for humanity, and a drive to utilize your inner powers and potentialities to love and to create. Jung stressed the implicit linkage with the spiritual and the unconscious. He wrote, "The conscious is only a part of the spiritual, and is never therefore capable of spiritual completeness: for that the indefinite expansion of the unconscious is needed" (quoted in Suzuki 1974, 27–28).

If you experience anxiety or fear in quiet solitude, don't worry. You simply have explored undiscovered dimensions of your deeper self. You will come to understand what fear primarily consists of—fear of the unknown self. In fact, I maintain that the experience of fear affirms that you have entered the right inward path. Go slow; as with physical exercise, you should gradually train your mind and emotions for this inward journey. As your self-knowledge increases, the aforementioned triadic scourge of inferiority—fear, anxiety, and aggression—should substantially diminish.

Most of us would like to know how to find our path in life, along with a sense of meaning, self-knowledge, and fulfillment. Shaman Don Juan Matus, who called his apprentices warriors, stressed (Castaneda 1974, 217–18) that "a warrior chooses to follow a path with heart. ... He knows that a path has heart when he is one with it, when he experiences a great peace and pleasure traversing its length." In a similar vein, Professor Campbell (in Patillo and Manchi 1988) upheld that, in a sacred place, we will experience the bliss and wonder of life. He presented a simple axiom by which his students might find their dreams, careers, and potentialities—*follow your bliss*. Campbell's formula to finding one's bliss in life is centered on asking oneself this question: "What do I want to pursue in life that would fill me with drive and passion?" The words of these two wise men have been a source of guidance, affirmation, and light in my own search for my path. Campbell (in Patillo and Manchi 1988) maintained that, as we transform ourselves, we simultaneously change the world and vice versa. Thus, in the matrix of a sacred place, dreams give birth and internal revolutions sprout. And when we transform the self, then we can help transform the world.

Do you seek romantic love? Self-knowledge stands as a precondition to intimacy and love because it instills self-confidence, the ability to trust, and the capacity to reveal oneself to another— intimacy. Furthermore, the confidence and security of self-knowledge enhances the ability for conflict resolution. Idealistically, males tend to seek a sexual goddess, and females seek a knight in shining armor. No person can meet all our emotional needs and demands, and a 50 percent divorce rate bears this out. These projected, idealistic sexual images actually mask the dormant potentialities that reside in you—the unconscious self. Self-knowledge can provide you with the capacity to experience a confident, vibrant, mature, wholesome, courageous, and sacred sexuality—yes, a radiant sexuality that emanates from the core of the authentic self. Often the root problem in romantic relationships or marriages consists of our irrational, infantile demands—our *shadow*. And beneath our infantile demands lurks the wounded child within us, who yearns for healing and wholeness. Usually, when we get angry or make demands, the reason stems from our overreaction in an attempt to protect the wounded child inside us. This powerful psychological phenomenon can contaminate relationships.

Consequently, in relationships, we often unconsciously attempt to use the bond of love to instinctively heal ourselves—the wounded child (read more about the self-cure instinct in chapters 5 and 17). That endeavor will be doomed to failure because relationships cannot heal our emotional wounds. Self-healing is a conscious action toward self-change and self-awareness. It is an autonomous act of purging one's emotional wounds from the past. Fromm (1967, 7) maintained that neurosis results from excessive anxiety due to our separateness from others and our failure to love our neighbor. Therefore, self-knowledge supplies the means to love with strength.

Yet for females there exists a slight variance from males in their struggle to break the chains of psychological and emotional dependency. The author Colette Dowling (1982, 21) emphasized that women must go inward to experience true "emancipation." Dowling wrote, *"Psychological dependency—the deep wish to be taken care of by others—is the chief force holding women down today. I call this 'The Cinderella Complex'—a network of largely repressed attitudes and fears that keeps women in a kind of half-light, retreating from the full use of their minds and creativity."*

Dowling's message is similar to that of Lomax. He stressed that authentic emancipation comes from *within*—an internal revolution. I maintain that a sacred place is the central command center from which we can prepare for the battles of adolescence and adulthood and launch an internal revolution. Over time, the practice of solitude can provide you with an invisible warrior's panoply of armor. And with this armor, you will be able to go inward and *exorcise*, if necessary, internal demons, ejecting false images of inferiority, shame, and guilt that have resulted from abuse and cultural, racial, ancestral, or gender intergenerational memories, as well as behavioral conditionings of submission and inferiority (see chapter 13). Adolescence initiates not only an internal battlefield but an external one as well. And these battles extend into adulthood. Both teens and adults may be assaulted by bullies and by an epidemic of narcissistic personalities (those who experience excessive self-importance). Bullies and narcissists project an attitude of superiority in athletics, sexuality, or academia, seeking to dominate psychologically in order to make others feel small and inferior.

I believe that a sacred place can be a unifying force for one's family and marriage because it abides as the place of inner authenticity. In a sacred place, one is psychologically centered and can become more self-aware and more able to release the anxieties, fears, and anger that can contaminate the bond of conjugal love and family ties. In short, our emotional baggage (shadows) infects bonds of love. And often those who are most vulnerable to our baggage are children. Jung (1991, 53) emphasizes that parents need to be consciously self-aware because, from birth, a child is psychologically merged with the psychology of their parents. This is a huge influence. Jung (39) wrote, "Children are so deeply involved in the psychological attitude of their parents that it is no wonder that most of the nervous disturbances of childhood can be traced back to a disturbed psychic atmosphere in the home." I include this quote not to impose blame or guilt but, on the contrary, to remind us to be aware of the powerful influence our unconscious can have on children and to reinforce Jung's (1989, 58) counsel to seek "ruthless self-knowledge." Although Jung's counsel is directed toward psychotherapists, I believe it rings true for parents and educators because we are all the guardians of the children on this earth. In the next chapter, I will present a technique called *recapitulation* that can assist one to release his or her emotional burden brought on by past painful memories, inferiorities, and so forth.

Over time in a sacred place, one's skills and newly emerged potentialities become refined, in the same way military training teaches the art of warfare. This psychological weaponry will empower you to unveil false social masks of superiority. You will be able to see through the Mr. Don Juan or Ms. Universe who brags of sexual conquests and popularity or the Mr. or Ms. Smarty-pants who boasts of omniscience or the Mr. and Ms. Olympia who vaunts athletic prowess as superior to everyone. You will discover that the behavior of these individuals and even their successes in athletics or academia or alleged sexual conquests simply comprise a *compensation* for their own internal shadow of *inferiority* (Adler 1979; Jung 1978, 8–9). An attitude of braggadocio is a form of psychological castration of others in order to feel superior. But it ultimately proves an act of futility and false power. Paying attention to the communication style of others will help you uncover these personality types. Narcissists tend to dominate personal or group interactions in a self-serving manner; they engage in monologues rather than healthy, reciprocal dialogue with others. We all have shadows, and in a sacred place, we can examine our shadows, become more aware of our pitfalls, and consciously intend to change our negative attitudes or behaviors (see chapter 13).

The author Joseph Campbell upheld that we can identify our shadow by thinking about the people we don't like. For me, the narcissistic person fuels my ire. Yet Campbell (2004, 73) and Jung (1977, 61) revealed that the shadow also retains a source of unrealized potentialities within us. For example, as with me, the narcissist person (one who has pseudoconfidence) provides a clue to what lacks in me—something that I need to develop—self-confidence (a dormant potentiality in me). In a similar vein, psychologist Frances Wickes (1978, 48–49) wrote, "Often we hate in others the thing which we fear in ourselves; or we hate because the other person raises to our consciousness some fault or inadequacy which we would prefer to have remain unconscious."

Some individuals might need a psychotherapist as a supportive guide to assist them in this deep exploration of the wounds of the past; complex emotions; and the vast, mysterious unconscious mind. Some people, unfortunately, have experienced more pain and trauma in life than others. Everyone possesses different strengths, pitfalls, and ways of coping. Psychotherapy contrasts to the ancient tribal tradition and ceremony of *storytellers*. This ceremony comprises the clients' own life story. The psychotherapist, the physician of the soul, guides the client in the reexamination of his or her life, and assisting the client as he or she moves back onto the path toward self-realization and achieving the dreams of his or her potentiality (Campbell 1999, 44). To find a competent psychotherapist, get recommendations from friends, relatives, or your local school's psychologist or social worker. Just like finding a good dentist or doctor, you can take advantage of others' experience of confidence and trust.

Author's Suggestions for Parents on a
Sacred Place for their Child

Parents can begin to use a sacred place at home with their children when the child reaches about age twelve. First, explain the purpose of a sacred place as a time for solitude to think about one's life, God, future goals, and one's strengths and pitfalls. Second, clarify that solitude is beneficial because the practice builds inner strength, such as self-understanding, patience, tolerance, improved concentration, and a sense of individuality. At a convenient time, like after dinner, you could participate as a family unit where everyone reads a book in silence; start slowly for five to ten minutes and work up to twenty minutes or more.

Other ideas include practicing total silence for thirty seconds and increasing the time each day until you reach five or ten minutes. The biggest difficulty is getting used to silence because it can create anxiety. Playing soft, soothing music can help create a tranquil mood. You can experiment with various exercises by consulting books, videos, TV programs, or websites on yoga, tai chi, or chi gung. A good opening exercise consists of a simple breathing technique where one takes a deep breath and holds it for three to five seconds and then slowly exhales; do three sets.

Two excellent techniques will improve both mental concentration and physical balance. (1) Stand an arm's length away from a wall. Stand on one foot with your arms perpendicular at a ninety-degree angle in front of you without touching the wall. Hold the position for fifteen to sixty seconds. Then switch legs. (2) Do the same technique but now close your eyes and place your arms at your side, using them to balance yourself as needed. The second technique is more difficult, but I do this daily and it undoubtedly provides a boost to my concentration and balance.

The above techniques all have some simple elements in common—relaxed breathing, light stretching, and meditative thought. Therefore, you can simply create exercises that work best for you and your family.

Key Points

- Spending time in one's sacred place in an activity like mediation or reading provides a haven from daily concerns. Solitude permits one to get psychologically and spiritually *centered* and to reflect on his or her goals, career, and God. Through solitude one can increase self-awareness, trust in his or her instinctive "inner voice," and understanding of human motives.

- If you encounter anxiety or fear in solitude, don't worry; this means that you have simply ventured into undiscovered dimensions of your deeper self. Then you will understand what fear primarily consists of—fear of the unknown self.

- Self-knowledge decreases fear, which enhances healthy romantic relationships because the psychoanalyst Fromm (1967, 75) emphasized that in a study on sexual problems of couples (frigidity and impotence), the cause lies not with, "A lack of knowledge of the right technique, but in the inhibitions which make it impossible to love. Fear of or hatred for the other sex are at the bottom of those difficulties." Moreover self-knowledge and a strengthened individuality prove essential in one's development and relationships since la Gorda, a female shaman (Castaneda 1991a, 132) maintained that, "An empty man [/woman] uses the completeness of a woman [/man] all the time."

- Jung (1991, 53) urges parents to be consciously self-aware because, from birth, a child is psychologically merged with the psychology of their parents.

- Our shadow consists of our infantile demands and inferiorities. Solitude can furnish us with a psychological suit of arms that will allow us to examine, work through, and expel these shadows; false beliefs of inferiority; abuse; and cultural, racial, ancestral, or gender intergenerational memories (see chapter 13) and, thereby, increase our self-awareness and personal growth.

Thirteen

Internal Revolution Tactic 3: Ejection of the False Image Within

Lomax maintained that an exorcism of sorts is needed to expel the demons of race—the inner socially constructed and inherited images of inferiority. However, an exorcism would also provide a means of healing for people who have experienced abuse, neglect, or abandonment, or for those who are plagued by inferiority, a condition that inflicts most of humanity. In a similar vein, many people could benefit from ousting the bothersome stored memories of failure and hurt. These memories may include experiences in school or romantic relationships. They may include times when we've behaved wrongly toward other people. In short, they include any situations about which we feel regret, shame, and guilt. Our regrets, remorse, and guilt can leave us with a heavy burden that can weigh us down and negatively affect our self-concept, our energy, and our drive to reach our goals. The purpose of this chapter is twofold. First, it attempts to provide parents and educators with information that will help them better understand how past experiences can hinder personal growth—that is, how experiences of emotional trauma or commonplace rejection can distort and taint one's self-concept. Second, a technique called recapitulation will be presented to show

how one can courageously self-heal his or her psychological and emotional wounds from the past.

Part of this *exorcism* comprises a cathartic release of grief as you let go of the past and move forward. This step is exemplified by Scrooge's journey through past Christmases. Yet for the likes of Marcus, Kurt, and Rafael, there often exists an invisible force, voice, demon, or monster within. Whenever someone experiences *domination*, whether sexual, physical, psychological, or cultural, he or she will likely experience a sense of powerlessness, inferiority, dehumanization, shame, guilt, and oppression by some unknown ubiquitous force. This force usually retains the silent, irrational belief or unconscious voice of the dominator—the sexual offender, an abusive parent, or the past white masters of the plantation culture, and so forth. Often victims will internalize or believe the false myth of cultural superiority/inferiority, or that they must perpetuate being objects for sexual exploitation or physical abuse. Consequently, they hold a false belief that shouts, *I am no good. I am unlovable, inferior, and a worthless piece of crap.* Like Rafael, people who have been abused feel plagued by pain, self-doubt, and *fear of the freedom to take responsibility* for their life. "The oppressed [or abused], having internalized the image of the oppressor [or abuser] and adapted his guidelines [false beliefs], are fearful of freedom. Freedom would require them to eject this image and replace it with autonomy and responsibility. Freedom is acquired by conquest, not by gift" (Freire 1970, 31).

Brazilian educator Paulo Freire suggests that this self-conquest will come only after an arduous journey. Our demons usually consist of memories or images that we have internalized and that have become part of our system of self-belief and identity. If we don't face and eject these false images or beliefs and seek the dream of freedom and authentic selfhood, a tendency to implode into self-destructive behaviors prevails. We can find this inner false image in the warehouse of our memory, where an event still evokes disturbing anxiety, fear, guilt, or anger in us. These experiences may include abuse, loss in romance or divorce, being ridiculed by a bully, or the vicious nicknames of childhood. Similarly, we may be haunted by memories of regretful behaviors enacted while intoxicated on alcohol or drugs. These images or memories can involve something that was done to us or something we did. Whatever they are, the memories are chains that prevent us from moving forward. Their voices tell us we are bad people, evoking shame, guilt, feelings of inferiority, and the "need" for emotional dependency. Within the false images, insidious and poignant thoughts of self-doubt echo, "I can't," and we believe we are incapable of self-change, success, or achieving our goals. Campbell (in Patillo and Manchi 1988) stressed that *self-doubt* is the embodiment of our inner dragon, and we must face the dragon (see chapter 16). To eject this image or memory means to release the hold these memories have on us.

It is very possible that Marcus or Kurt might believe and act out the false myths (the guidelines or beliefs of the oppressor) that their experiences instilled in them. Kurt might become a violent sexual offender. Either boy could become a school dropout, unemployed and prone to criminality, violence, and prison. "The 'fear of freedom' which afflicts the oppressed, a fear which may equally well lead them to desire the role of oppressor or bind them to the role of oppressed, should be examined" (Freire 1970, 31).

If we don't eject false beliefs about racial inferiority and memories of abuse or personal failure, then the false beliefs and memories will maintain power over us and we will reinforce the lie that we are *submissive* or *dependent*. Dr. Albert Ellis, a cognitive psychoanalyst, successfully used rational reasoning with clients so they could extinguish their neurotic false belief systems. The journey on which Marcus, Kurt, or any of us must embark in order to face these inner wounds is arduous. In fact, in may seem insurmountable. But the human spirit is resilient and strong. Lomax upheld that there subsists only one place to go—*inward*—the hero path.

Simon embarked on this journey when he decided that he would go up the mountain to discover whether or not the beast really existed. The boys became horrified and dismayed, but Simon (Golding 1954, 128) retorted, "What else is there to do?" In short, Simon suggested that, in the journey of life, we must face our anxieties and fears, and in this unknown darkness rests the light of self-knowledge and our potentialities. Later, Simon stealthily trekked up the mountain to visit the beast and discovered that the beast was only a dead human parachutist—a false belief, an illusion.

Recapitulation

Various visualization or imagery techniques claim to release the negative effects of false images or negative memories that are the source of our feelings of inferiority, anxieties, fears, anger, guilt, and regrets. Over the years, I have experimented with about a half a dozen of these techniques proposed by the likes of neuropsychologists, psychoanalysts, and social workers. One stands out as the most effective. Yaqui Indian shaman, Don Juan Matus, advocated what he termed *recapitulation* (Castaneda 2000, 142–59). Professor Campbell (in Patillo and Manchi 1988) explained that a shaman has a primary function as the tribal priest; however, occasionally the shaman plays a secondary role as the tribal psychoanalyst, particularly when a young adolescent becomes psychologically traumatized by visions. The shaman knows instinctively that the youngster has experienced "the call" to duty as a shaman. So the shaman assists the young male or female to adapt, learn, and integrate these psychological forces through solitude, fasting, chanting of songs, meditation, and prayers. In our modern parlance, this youngster's psychological trauma would likely be diagnosed as schizophrenia, along with a different cultural response for a cure (see Campbell 1988a, chapter 10, "Schizophrenia—The Inward Journey").

Recapitulation consists of recollecting and writing the names of people and events from one's life in quiet solitude, somewhere like a sacred place. It helps to organize this list structurally along stages of life, whether schools, jobs, living locations, and so forth; one should organize the list and recapitulate beginning from the present and then moving into the past in an orderly fashion. Attempt to recall as much detail as possible from the interactions and feelings experienced.

Second, while reviewing each name and event on the list, focus on breathing; move your head from side to side in a slow, fanning motion, and inhale while moving from right to left and exhale in the return rightward movement. Breathing is important because the ancient shamans believed the breath has a "magical life-giving function" (Castaneda 2003, 149). This belief in the importance of breathing plays an important role with other practices such as yoga, Zen Buddhism, or chi gung. Deep breathing triggers the parasympathetic nervous system (the natural "rest" and "digest" system while we sleep or eat) so blood circulation flows through the body's organs and glands—a form of exercise. In short, deep breathing puts the mind-body in self-healing mode. Moreover, modern research shows that varying breathing exercises trigger neuropeptides (molecules of emotion) in the brain stem and move quickly through the entire cerebrospinal fluid in order to maintain balance (Pert 2003, 186–87). Pert (187) emphasized that these peptides in the respiratory center, "may provide the scientific rationale for the powerful healing effects of consciously controlled breath patterns." Eventually, you should narrow down the list to key events in your life.

Don Juan explained "that as we *recapitulate* our lives, all the debris ... comes to the surface. We realize our inconsistencies, our repetitions, but something in us puts up a tremendous resistance to *recapitulating*" (Castaneda 2000, 148). In short, recapitulation removes the psychological and emotional garbage we've stored and enables us to become more self-aware of the essential patterns and composition of influential events from our life (158).

If we truly intend to recapitulate but maintain a prolonged resistance then a stupendous event could likely occur in order to open the pathway to recapitulate. Don Juan stressed that shamans believed, "The road [for recapitulation] is free only after a gigantic upheaval, after the appearance on our screen of the memory of an event that shakes our foundations with its terrifying clarity of detail. It's the event that drags us to the actual moment that we lived it" (Castaneda 2000, 148–49).

The ancient shamans called this momentous occurrence *the usher*. I had been resisting recapitulation for many months, and then out of the blue "the usher" happened to me in June 2011: I had some medical lab tests taken at a medical center because I was absolutely 100 percent sure I had a medical problem. On health issues, I am a bona fide neurotic, so I was in a state of high anxiety and panic. Well, when I picked up my results the next day, the tests had come out negative! I thought that was totally impossible. I insisted on seeing and speaking with the lab technician who had examined the specimen. The Filipina medical technician appeared to be highly qualified and competent, and when I described the specimen, she emphatically said that she observed nothing and the examination additionally proved negative. The experience was so bizarre and surreal; I was dumbfounded because I could not deny the technician's honest, objective, and professional appraisal, which consequently shook the foundations of my reality and, hence, rocked my world! I must have appeared to the technician like some deranged lunatic.

A nanosecond later, I knew that it was *the usher*. I promptly returned home and began in earnest my list for recapitulation and have not stopped since. Of course, I had a second examination, and to my chagrin and relief it came out negative.

I had immediately realized, too, that my *fear*—specifically a phobia from childhood—had created the delusion of alleged illness. I believe if we truly *intend* to engage in this pivotal self-healing activity of recapitulation, then the powerful unconscious (the deeper undiscovered potential self) triggers the usher when we are ready for it. Remember that Jung and Freud said humans possess an instinct of self-cure (see chapter 5). I believe this is a most powerful human instinct that we can harness through such activities as spending time in a sacred place, recapitulation, and dream work (see chapter 15). Meanwhile, we often underutilize this self-healing instinct or divert it into excessive, avoidant, and indulgent activities, such as overworking, alcohol and drug, risky sexual behavior, escapist consumerism, prolonged technology usage, overeating, and so forth.

I mention my own usher experience to demonstrate that, if the usher happens to you, it is likely related to some past psychological event. My fear actually related to my psychological relationship with my parents and the powerful attachment and separation experiences of childhood that everyone experiences. Remember that Jung (1989, 182) emphasized that everyone has mother and father complexes (see chapter 10). But the real question lies in what task is being avoided. This time, I had been avoiding the instinctive self-healing act of recapitulation.

The usher parallels the rare petrifying messengers in our dreams as exemplified by Scrooge's terror when the Ghost of Christmas Past arrived (see chapter 9), or as when I experienced my nightmares of 2000 (see chapter 10), or when the wise old man Archetype appeared in my dream with a warning and created profound anxiety and panic in me (see chapter 15, "Dream One"). The fear functions, whether in a dream or in the usher, to awaken and move us toward change, healing, self-realization, expanded consciousness, and personal growth. However, the usher occurs not in an unconscious dream but in awake consciousness, which compounds our utter fright and turmoil. But as one becomes more attuned to his or her unconscious through solitude, recapitulation, and dream work, one's level of consciousness or self-awareness expands. And soon one can *perceive* beyond the surface of things, whether in oneself, in their children, with students, or in the environment. Remember that Jung (1991, 51) stressed that the unconscious is never at rest but in continual interplay with the conscious.

When these haphazard yet coincidental occurrences of external phenomena produce deep *meaning* internally for an individual—like the usher had for me—Jung coined such incidents as *synchronicities* (Jung et al. 1968, 226–27); in contrast, others like the shaman Don Juan Matus referred to these events as omens. These synchronistic occurrences happen more frequently than we realize, but usually we don't notice them because of a lack of self-awareness. Dr. M. L. von Franz emphasized that synchronistic events occur in one's life at important stages of their individuation process (226–27).

According to Dr. Jolande Jacobi, Jung displayed that one's dreams often directly relate to the synchronistic event (Jung et al. 1968, 357–58). A trick to increase awareness of synchronicities is to be consciously aware of the crucial linkage of the event with dream symbols (e.g., an animal, a bird, a tree, or archetypes). Personally,

I find this advice profoundly accurate; my experience affirms that synchronicities usually consist of an *affirmation* that one stands on the correct path. The synchronistic experience always increases my confidence and motivation in my search and personal growth. In fact, years after my personal crisis in 2000, I realized the synchronistic connections with the three individuals whose words of wisdom helped provide me with a plan of action. My friend Jake mirrored the dream figure of the wise old man. The writer Carol and my friend Ann both personified the earth mother archetype (see chapter 15, "Dream Archetypes").

On the other hand, I have experienced synchronicities as warnings; for example, a few times when I have been in an irritable mood—my *shadow*—suddenly I have observed a person who mirrors the same cantankerous behavior. Immediately, I have understood the message and refocused, getting in command of my emotions. So whenever I experience this powerful mysterious force of the unconscious and the universe, whether in meditation, dreams, or in the usher, I recall what the shaman Don Juan Matus stressed to his apprentice, "Don't worry. … You're not going crazy. What you felt was the gentle tap of *infinity*" (Castaneda 2000, 73). Remember too that Jung (1990a, 106) emphasized that what we really fear is the magical effect of the unconscious (see chapter 1).

Don Juan stressed that recapitulation releases energy entrapped within us because the ancient shamans believed that exhalation of breath *ejects* "the foreign energy left in the individual during the interaction being recapitulated and the inhalation returns energy that was left behind during the interaction" (Castaneda 2003, 148–49). In addition, Don Juan emphasized lots of walking as one writes his or her list of events because walking triggers the memory process; the ancient shamans in Mexico believed that, in the back of the legs, resides the *sensation* storehouse for one's personal history (149). This ancient wisdom implies a mind-body connection of thought and emotion that modern neuroscience (see chapter 2) has researched, tested, and validated. Moreover, Don Juan's advice stands commensurate with the common medical recommendation for bodily movement or exercise to enhance one's mental and emotional well-being. A cautionary note: if the process of recapitulation becomes psychologically and emotionally overwhelming, one may need to seek the services of a psychotherapist as a guide to explore and work through one's past.

One should recapitulate the most significant events until the intense emotional content has been exhausted. The second phase to recapitulation is called *fluidity*. During this phase, one recapitulates not in any specific order or sequence but spontaneously or, as Don Juan suggested, "Let the spirit decide. Be silent, and then get to the event the spirit points out" (Castaneda 2003, 150). I expand this principle and recapitulate not just in my sacred place in the morning and evening but for a quick minute or so before I leave home so I can be better attuned with my mind-body-spirit as I experience the many distractions of the day.

The incorporation of recapitulation has been one of the most important, beneficial, liberating, and empowering psychological-emotional-spiritual techniques in my life. For example, from recapitulating my shadow behaviors, I have increasingly experienced that, when I get angry, I don't get as consumed by my emotions (in other words, by the angry boy within) as I usually do. I simply get angry but without the "emotional baggage" or intensity of the wounded child within—an extremely liberating and enlightening experience. In short, recapitulation is a most effective self-healing activity and quasi *rite of purification* for internal psychological and emotional cleansing.

Moreover, I keep creating new ways to utilize this powerful technique. For example, I inject (inhale) potentialities that I want in my life, such as increased energy, patience, creativity, flexibility, and so forth. Meanwhile, I eject (exhale) shadows of irritability, self-importance, rigidity, anxiety, fear, self-doubt, inferiority, castration anxieties and fears, indulging in sexual and aggressive projections. As Don Juan stressed, recapitulation of one's life never ends (Castaneda 2003, 147). Through recapitulation and conscious intention, we can break free from the hold of false beliefs, past memories and history, and the fear of the self, of our emotions, and the unconscious.

I think recapitulation produces such a positive and seemingly magical effect because the breathing combined with conscious *intention* puts the mind-body in accord with the powerful instinct of self-cure (see chapters 5 and 17) that exists within us. In short, recapitulation is as intentional and instinctive act of self-healing.

Campbell summed that we retain one responsibility in life—to seek and find our human potentiality; we must take the *inward heroic path*. I maintain that adolescence initiates this journey throughout the rest of our lives. Through recapitulation of one's life events in a sacred place, one can successfully engage in this conquest and exorcise one's demons, such as feelings of inferiority.

Author's Suggestions for Parents

After parents complete their initial recapitulation and feel confident about the benefits of this technique, I suggest they decide whether their teenager would benefit from recapitulation if the teen expresses interest in doing so. Parents would need to thoroughly explain this chapter to the youth or read it together. The difficult part of recapitulation is the willingness of the individual to write the list of events from their life. The head fanning technique itself provides a sense of release.

Key Points

- Michael Lomax proposed that a quasi exorcism is needed to oust the demons of race; that is, the inner socially constructed and inherited images of inferiority.
- For children such as Marcus and Kurt, an invisible force, voice, or monster often endures within. Through cruel incidences of domination—whether sexual, physical, psychological, or cultural—the individual will likely experience a sense of powerlessness, inferiority, dehumanization, shame, guilt, and oppression by some unknown force.

- We need to confront and expel these false images or beliefs and seek true emancipation and genuine selfhood; otherwise, internalized fear and inferiority can spark self-destructive behaviors. People who have experienced domination risk transmuting their future roles from victims to abusers.

- Recapitulation consists of remembering and writing the names of people and events from one's life in solitude. One should recapitulate the most pertinent events listed until the intense emotional content has been dispelled. Deep breathing and walking help in the process of recapitulation.

- Recapitulation—like a *rite of purification*—banishes the psychological and emotional refuse stored throughout our lives. Recapitulation generates such a positive and mystic effect because the breathing united with conscious *intention* puts the mind-body in harmony with the potent instinct of self-cure.

- If we sincerely desire to recapitulate but resist, then a breathtaking event could happen that would open us to recapitulation. The ancient shamans called this occasion *the usher*.

- The usher may come in the form of a petrifying dream messenger in nightmares, as when archetypal figures bring warnings by producing acute anxiety and fear in order to awaken and move us toward change, healing, self-realization, expanded consciousness, and personal growth—like the incident at the radiology lab.

- Jung referred to these random but meaningful incidents as *synchronicities*.

FOURTEEN

Internal Revolution Tactic 4: Awareness of the Death Instinct

The purpose of this chapter is to provide parents and educators an increased awareness of the instinct of aggression within us. After an explanation of the death instinct, the chapter will present examples of the behaviors that result from aggression to aid the reader to become more aware of its presence within themselves and in others, as they observe their relationships with children, teens, and all of humanity. I maintain that, through this increased awareness and an understanding of the death instinct, we can embrace this force as an inner voice and guide that will teach us what aspects of our lives we need to let go (let die). Then we can move forward in our growth, self-healing, and independence with a sense of rebirth and resurrection (see chapter 17).

In the concluding paragraph in *Civilization and It's Discontents*, Freud (1962a, 111) wrote ominously, "The fateful question for the human species seems to be for me whether and to what extent their cultural development will succeed in mastering the disturbance of their communal life by the human instinct of aggression and self-destruction."

Freud presented modern civilizations a dire caveat when it comes to our human instinct of aggression and self-destruction—the death instinct. This mysterious, volatile, and powerful tour de force inside us should not be denied but understood and respected. On the one hand, the aggressive instinct has a positive function; it is part of our survival mechanism of self-defense when under threat (Lorenz 1969, 40). On the other hand, the aggressive instinct can boomerang or implode and inflict an insidious, destructive, and self-sabotaging dynamism (the death instinct) and be projected outwardly into acts of violence or turned inward into self-destructive behaviors like suicide.

Freud (1962b, 30) did not write at length on the death instinct, but he succinctly said its function "is to lead organic life back into the inanimate state." He suggests that humans possess this inner dualistic tension with the life and death forces within them. These instincts can interact and even unify in mysterious and contradictory ways, but the life instinct generally is dominate. On the one hand, in our daily observations of the world, we see killings and war among individuals and nations. Moreover, there exist acts of suicide by individuals or, as Freud warned, the potential of humanity's self-destructive use of weapons of mass destruction. On the other hand, we can observe the seemingly paradoxical unity of the life and death instincts when a mother sacrifices her life to save her child in a burning house or when a soldier sacrifices his life to save his comrades in battle. Furthermore, this dualistic tension often surfaces in romance and family life with its immense love (life instinct) and bonding, and yet conflict can suddenly turn love to anger or even hate and acts of violence (death instinct).

We can observe this polarity of tension between the forces of life and death in our cultures and in our individual lives. In agrarian or planting tribal cultures, mythologies usually center on death and rebirth; the planting seed must be buried (die) in the ground so food for life can sprout forth. As I noted in chapter 1, adolescence marks the death of childhood and a rebirth into adulthood. During my drug abuse years of late adolescence, I consciously said to myself at age twenty-one that I was not going to turn age twenty-three and still be living an irresponsible, adolescent party life. I had a plan to let it go and seek my life's purpose, but I deliberately delayed this action for two years because I wanted to exit with a prolonged last hurrah of excessive alcohol and high-risk drug use. My intention was to burn myself out so I could let it all go. Of course, this did not work out exactly according to my intended script. I had to face the consequences of the enormous psychological and emotional adjustments to an alcohol and drug-free lifestyle, a temporary separation from my friends, and the difficulty of concentration in reading and studying in the university. But in my own idiosyncratic way, I sought the *death* of my adolescence and a *rebirth/resurrection* into responsible adulthood. My instincts (life and death instincts) subconsciously conveyed to me that I had to create a "death" of my present life in order to find my future "life purpose."

In my experience with adolescents, I often observed self-destructive behaviors, such as with Rafael, or when a senior student, Rich, quit school six weeks before he was set to graduate. Furthermore, this phenomenon of potential self-destruction eclipsed with the suicides of Liza and John, as well as with my own episode of depression and suicidal ideation. These experiences compelled me to seek to understand this mysterious force of the death instinct within our human nature.

Freud astutely points out that this force of life and death (instincts) emanates within us. My aim in this chapter (also see chapter 17) is to show that, through awareness of this inner death instinct, we can embrace this force as an inner voice, ally, and guide that will teach us what aspects of our lives we need to let go (let die). And we can move forward in our human growth, self-awareness, and independence with a sense of rebirth and resurrection. The psychological-emotional-spiritual armor developed in a sacred place and through the activity of recapitulation provides a means of becoming more attuned to our emotions and instincts and better able to manage the dynamism of the death instinct if it arises. Other useful tools, such as a dream work and journal writing, will be presented in part 4.

The aggressive instinct can boomerang and inflict an insidious, destructive, and self-sabotaging dynamism that can creep up in our lives frequently in the most subtle situations which we need to be aware. Possibly the most universal human experience of this phenomenon abides in The Bad Day Syndrome.

Have you ever experienced a bad day? Most people have, and I sure have. And a bad day can turn into a nightmare. One of my bad days went like this: On a November weekday morning, I abruptly awoke in a panic and glanced at my alarm clock, which read 7:15 a.m.—damn, I had forgotten to set the clock for 6:00 a.m. Immediately I feel irritable, not the way to start my day. As I hurried to the bathroom, I banged my toe on the bed frame—ouch, sob! My anger rose. Not only did my toe hurt, more importantly, I didn't have thirty minutes to read and reflect in my sacred place, a daily ritual that functions like a self-imposed psychological *protection charm*. As I prepared to make coffee, I noticed the empty coffee jar. Stupid me! I had forgotten to buy coffee last night. While rapidly shaving, I cut my chin and blood spurt—damn! As I drank a cup of tea with the TV on, a live news bulletin reported a terrorist bombing and displayed horrific visual scenes of blood and body parts everywhere—awh! Now I couldn't get these hideous images out of my thoughts. Suddenly, my mind-body felt overrun by irrational thoughts, anxieties, and fears. *Maybe my nightly walks are too dangerous*, the thoughts said. *Maybe I should not travel to Latin America this summer. The world is self-destructing!*

When I went outside to my car, I saw that six inches of fresh snow had fallen—damn! As I drove cautiously to Cougarville, a car suddenly sped past my left and then cut me off. I yelled, "Whoa, you idiot!" And then I gave the jerk some horn.

The driver slowed down and flipped me off.

Now I was really pissed off. "F you too, dude! Up yours too, pal." I was now in a road rage situation that could easily spin out of control.

I finally caught myself and backed off. I cooled down and got in command of my emotions. Then I recalled what Professor Joseph Campbell (1988a, 148) refers to as the *doctrine of mutual arising*, a Buddhist concept that holds that all of life flows as *mutually arising*, so no one is at fault for anything that happens—even if a knucklehead cuts me off. Besides, I was equally a participant. I had gotten myself into this specific situation by being late, rushing, and allowing my emotions to get worked up and out of control. *Mutual arising* is as an intriguing concept that makes us responsible for all our interactions.

When I arrived at my office, I shut the door and spent a few minutes in an impromptu sacred place to reflect and get myself centered. I used a breathing technique—a two-count inhale and a four-count exhale. I stopped berating myself for my human errors and evaluated the snowballing events that had led to the chaotic morning. I decided to redeem the remainder of the day. Stress breaks down our physical and psychological defenses, and in a sacred place, we can restore our emotional, physical, and psychological equilibrium.

Understanding Self-Sabotaging Behaviors

Let's examine the powerful and insidious manifestation of the death instinct within me on my bad day. Some general emotional, cognitive, and behavioral clues exist when the death instinct surfaces and might cause havoc:

1. First, forgetfulness—I forgot to get coffee and to set my alarm. In short, this displayed a subtle self-sabotaging behavior that can be seen as a self-imposed, dark magic jinx.

2. Externally, I became accident prone. I banged my toe due to impulsiveness, and this can be interpreted as self-punitive behavior—punishing myself for my forgetfulness. In fact Lorenz (1969, 237) wrote, "It has been proved that accident-proneness may result from repressed aggression." This incident shouts a warning—*Hey, slow down, relax, and get centered.*

3. Internally, the influx of anxiety and irrational fear as I watched the media's images of terror and death created havoc on my limbic (emotional) brain, particularly the amygdala (the inner warning system) that ignites the autonomic nervous system's flight (fear) or fight (aggression) response (Goleman 1996, 19–21). However, when we can stop, self-examine, and change our emotional responses, we can actually strengthen the neural circuitry of our emotional brain to better control the amygdala's potential to overrun the rational brain (260). Moreover, research shows that the act of *reframing* a volatile situation is a most effective means of appeasing anger (66). We should wear a psychological protective shield to hinder the toxicity of fear, terror, and death that permeates the airwaves and often feeds anxiety and fear. By simply listening to or reading the news, one can lessen the intensity of emotions evoked because generally the visual images on television or video tend to increase its poignancy.

4. Irritability, anger, bad mood, expletives, and aggression signal the loss of command of our emotions. And the wounded child just may be unleashed "spontaneously" into aggressive hostility, conflict, and violence.

As Lorenz (1969, 47) stressed, the danger of aggression abounds in its *spontaneity*. Maintaining self-control can be difficult at this stage; it seems as if the wounded child exploits this crisis and shouts, *Yes, I am angry and have the right to act out aggressively (death instinct)!* So the wounded child, our shadow, remains fixated in childhood and refuses to grow up. But when the wounded child gets angry and aggression sparks, the shadowy, wounded child and the death instinct seem to unify and transmogrify into a powerful, destructive force.

The importance of awareness of this subconscious dynamism of the death instinct cannot be understated. Other possible early warning symptoms of its presence include conditions of stress, boredom, melancholy, irritability, lack of concentration, anger, pessimism, a critical attitude of others, gossip, excessive passivity, victimization behaviors, an excessive stance of compliance or dependency, and so forth.

Aggression and the death instinct can implode into acts of self-sabotage and self-destruction. But the process of human deterioration and the implosion of the death instinct can bellow a final caveat, since this road may ultimately lead to the poignant self-destructive act of suicide (see chapters 10 and 17).

Author's Suggestions for Parents and Educators

I think parents and educators can assist teens to become more aware of this dynamism of humanity's self-destructive or self-sabotaging nature—the death instinct—whenever a *teachable moment* arises. Teachable moments may include televised news about personal suicide, a suicidal mass killing, or a suicide bomber. Parents or educators can simply open discussion by asking, "Why did this person do this? What do you think really needed to die, symbolically speaking, in this person's life or in his or her culture? What kind of resurrection or change seems to be necessary in the person's life or in the culture at large?"

Other teachable moments may include incidents of potentially self-destructive behaviors being reported in the media or children participating locally in self-damaging activities like gang membership, truancy, and dropping out of school or high-risk activities like car racing. In the context of the discussion, I suggest that parents and educators use expressions like *beat himself up*, *self-punishment*, and *set herself up*, as well as terms like *victimhood*, *victimization*, *self-sabotage*, and *self-destructive*. These discussions can aid teens to increase their self-awareness and emotional intelligence. See chapter 17 for further discussion on the death instinct.

Key Points

- Individuals can harness the death instinct as an internal guide to show them what needs to change or "die" in their lives and help move them forward in self-awareness and personal growth.
- Freud warned that cultures need to understand and master the human aggressive instinct.
- Our aggressive drive can be used positively for self-defense, but it can sometimes arise out of the blue as a self-destructive force, like in a "bad day" episode where one mishap snowballs into a series of blunders. In such occurrences, the emotional brain suddenly dominates the rational brain; however, we can reduce the charged emotions by consciously calming down with deep breathing and *reframing* logically the precipitating events. Some precursors of the death instinct's presence include forgetfulness, accident proneness, irritability, anger, bad mood, abusive language, and aggression.
- Parents and educators can help teens to be more self-aware of the death instinct when *teachable moment*s surface. These moments may include media coverage of issues like personal suicide or mass killings or when local teens behave in self-damaging behaviors like in truancy or gang membership.

PART FOUR

Self-Analysis for an Internal Revolution

Part 4 continues to focus on methods for an internal revolution—a transformation that includes strengthening our individuality through increased self-awareness and self-knowledge. But in this part, we will gain an even deeper understanding of self-analysis and work on refining our ability to gain personal insight and growth. Through increased self-awareness, we can develop a deeper sense of attunement with our emotions and instincts, which harmoniously unifies the mind, body, and spirit. As a result, we can harness and capitalize upon the wisdom of the unconscious and the human instinct of self-cure (see chapter 5) for self-healing. We will examine three techniques that target specific aspects of our nature. Dream work focuses on the unconscious, journal writing allows us to work on the intellect and our emotions, and understanding the death instinct targets our mind-body-spirit. Through these techniques, we can further solidify our own autonomous psychological-emotional-spiritual armor and establish an internal fortress of self-power, self-healing, personal growth, and increased emotional intelligence.

This section will include suggestions on how parents can assist their teenager to begin dream work and journal writing. Chapter 17, "Understanding the Death Instinct," will provide additional information about how parents and educators can help adolescents become more aware of self-sabotaging behaviors. This chapter will show how the death instinct can be a major catalyst for interpersonal conflict, academic failure, dropping out of school, incarceration, and even suicide. Parents, educators, and teens need to be aware and understand this powerful human instinct and learn to harness its positive potentiality.

FIFTEEN

Self-Analysis 1: Dreams—the Emissary of the Unconscious

We often face moments in our lives, be these moments during adolescence or adulthood, when we need the support and counsel of a wise mentor. A mentor can be a parent, teacher, writer, guidance counselor, psychotherapist, friend, or even an acquaintance. The sagacious words or advice of these guides can evoke aha moments that can redirect and change our lives. For example, through their books Campbell and Jung have been erudite teachers for me and have changed and steered my life in profound ways. During my episode of depression and suicidal ideation, the words of wisdom from three wise friends helped bring me clarity and allowed me to guide my life toward a new path. Through this experience, I discovered a deeper confidence in a most important yet often underutilized mentor that everyone has access to—the messenger of dreams, otherwise known as the wisdom of the unconscious.

An assault from my unconscious in February 2000 awakened me and helped me embrace my unconscious (my dreams) as a reliable and perspicacious teacher and guide for my individuation and self-healing.

In this chapter, I intend to provide the reader with the basic tools to self-analyze their dreams by understanding the symbolic meaning of archetypal figures and dream symbols. Jung named these archetypal figures the shadow, anima/animus, wise old man/ earthly mother, the child, and the trickster. I will present six of my dreams for instructional purposes to help the reader understand archetypes and symbols as a tool for analyzing your own dreams. Freud called this activity *dream work*. Our dreams are a resource and inner teacher that can increase our self-knowledge and individuation. The better we understand our dreams, the less fear we will have of the unconscious (in other words of the undiscovered self) and of our emotions. Dream symbols provide clues through which both adolescents and adults can discover their unique identities, goals, path in life, and potentialities; obtain psychological and emotional balance; increase self-awareness and self-knowledge; and experience psychological and emotional healing. Dream work is an adventure like a treasure hunt. But the treasure that awaits is accessing the wisdom of the unconscious as a guide in our lives toward self-realization, self-healing, and fulfillment.

The more poignant a dream the more likely it is that we have failed to listen and our conscious is trying to get our attention (Jung et al. 1968, 34). We should embrace the messages of our dreams for two important reasons. First, recall that Jung and Freud (see chapter 5) believed that humans have an *instinct* for self-cure or self-healing. In addition, Jung referred to the *circle* as a universal symbol for wholeness and healing (see chapter 5). The circle symbol arises often in dreams because it represents the totality of the self and healing. So our dreams are a means by which we can self-heal. Second, Jung (1990a, 44) also explained that archetypes comprise "the unconscious images of the instincts themselves, in other words, that they are *patterns of instinctual behavior.*" Therefore, by listening to our dreams and instincts—the deep inner voice—we can harness the healing potential from the archetypal energies within us. Similarly, Campbell (in Patillo and Manchi 1988) summed that, by reflecting on these archetypal symbols, we can awaken their powers to function in our lives.

Metaphorically, dreams create images like a computer game, but the screen is one's internal memory and the mind's creative and imaginary capacity. The power source is not an implanted microchip but energy from the vast, mysterious unconscious mind. Just as a computer program provides a tool for instruction, dreams can reveal an internal teacher, a helpful guide, and an occasional wise tenacious bodyguard, who warns us if we detour from the path of growth, individuation, and independence. A visual war game gives us an imagery of adventure, challenge, camaraderie, and the vicarious or virtual sense of power; however, this projective gratification from war games actually disguises or masks the projective powers that lie dormant inside us. Therefore, dreams are the source of authentic power and provide a means to discover one's identity and unrealized potentialities within.

Freud, Jung, and Campbell believed that dreams come from the human psyche and imagination just like myths, legends, and fairy tales. But as Campbell (1989, 78) emphasized, personal dreams reflect the dreamer's story—one's personalized myth. So dreams are the means of communication between the conscious and unconscious systems. Jung et al. (1968, 38) suggests that the dreamer stands as the central interpreter of his or her dreams and that dreams do not have any fixed meaning and every symbol can have at least two interpretations (Jung 1989, 236–37). Freud (1964, 34) maintained there are three kinds of dreams—wish fulfillments, anxiety, and punishment dreams. Freud (13) suggests that remnants from the prior day usually exist within dreams.

The trick to recalling your dreams rests in the conscious intention of wanting to. Therefore, *before* lying down to bed, make a conscious notation or tell your unconscious that you want to remember your dreams and that you would like to have dreams about discovering your potentialities and goals. Ask for guidance in matters of relationships, for direction of life, in learning how to change your behavioral pitfalls or shadows, how to heal your emotional wounds, and so forth. Be sure to have a pen and notebook next to your bed so you can begin a dream journal. Most people do not remember their dreams every night, but the important aspects rests in your *intention*, which the unconscious will honor.

When you recall a dream, write down as much detail as possible; include people, places, animals, shapes, colors, and so forth: Freud (1998, 311) called what we remember from a dream the *manifest content*. Second, write down all the emotions that the dream evoked in you since these emotions provide the clues for interpretation. Freud called this *latent content*. Emotions are the vehicle to understanding our dreams, the deeper self, and the unconscious because emotions are messages from the mind-body and unconsciousness to take action—e-motion (Goleman 1996, 6, 60).

Review what you wrote to make sure of the accuracy or to add any other content or emotion. You can review the dream the next day and analyze its meaning. However, if the dream is particularly poignant, I prefer to wait a few days or weeks before I reread the dream in order to get some emotional distance from the dream so I can objectively analyze it better.

Another good trick for dream work is to make your own personal mandala (Campbell in Patillo and Manchi 1988). Simply draw a circle on a piece of paper and arrange the energy systems in your life. These may include family, career, romance, friends, goals, sports, hobbies, and interests. This exercise will help you get *centered* and focus on your goals and priorities. This exercise reinforces your *intention* of using dreams for personal growth and self-realization, making it all the more likely that your dreams will provide the information you seek. Eventually you can add to your mandala significant symbols from your dreams that have become meaningful to you. For years, I have drawn the lightning bolt symbol from dreams four and five—see below—on my mandala daily, and I continued to experience its active potency in my life.

Dream Self-Analysis

Since late 2000, I began to experience changes in my life and an ascent from the depths of depression. I felt compelled to thoroughly comprehend the messages my unconscious was sending through nightmarish dreams, anxiety, depression, and suicidal ideation. Uncomfortable emotions of anxiety and fear prove deceptive and can mask deeper issues, but the more we experience and understand our emotional life, the more we grow in self-knowledge and emotional intelligence. My unconscious was assaulting me because I had repressed and denied my dream to write a book on adolescence. As Jung (1990b, 62) summed, *"The unconscious is nature, which never deceives: only we deceive ourselves."*

My dream to write emerged in the mid-1990s when I gave lectures (group work) on adolescent psychology to students at Cougarville. I explained psychology with language that students could understand, and they astonished me with their comprehension. But I failed to take specific action upon my dream to write; I procrastinated and placed writing on my "to do list"—someday. In the same vein, a specific event triggered the nightmares in February 2000 when I traveled to a weekend job fair in Cedar Rapids, Iowa, where I searched for positions at international schools. Consequently, I *consciously* made a choice with the *intention* to take a different direction in my life and not write. The nightmares began in Iowa.

Nightmares or dream dragons function, as Campbell (in Patillo and Manchi 1988) maintained, to "open us up" because of our resistance, denial, and repression. I feared change. Jung (1977, 21) summarized that dreams function as "the emissary of the unconscious, whose task it is to reveal the secrets that are hidden from the conscious mind, and this it does with astounding completeness." Meanwhile, Freud (1998, 647) referred to dreams as the royal road to the unconscious.

Below I will present six dreams in sequence of their occurrence as an instructional guide for self-analysis of one's dreams. The first two dreams reflect the inner turmoil, repression, and denial I experienced in early 2000. The latter four dreams show how I moved out of my depression and began to experience a new dawn in my life.

Dream One

In late March 2000, I wrote in my dream journal, "In a backyard of a house, an old blind man's leashed dog craves to pursue me. They exit the yard, and he takes the dog for a walk, but the dog gets loose and attacks me. I throw rocks at the dog, and it runs home afraid."

Interpretation: Years later, I can examine these dreams more objectively. The house symbolizes my ego field of consciousness. The old blind man symbolizes what Jung (1990a, 37) called the wise old man archetype, which represents the authority of the one whom, "like the anima … pierces the chaotic darkness of brute life with the light of meaning. He is the enlightener, the master and teacher." The wise old man represents, "knowledge, reflection, insight, wisdom, and intuition … and readiness to help" (222). Therefore, the old man told me that I was not "loyal" (dogs often represent loyalty) to myself, dreams, and potentialities. Moreover, I was "blinded" to this message from my unconscious, and I was throwing away my potentialities for self-realization and self-healing (the small circular rocks symbolize the child archetype who represents potentiality, healing, light, and expanded consciousness—see below). Blind and afraid, I was not "seeing" the source of my resistance because of fear. My defenses and internal controls had weakened while the forces of the unconscious emerged unleashed (the dog). Dogs also represent guardians of treasure (Jung 1990b, 372). For more data on the female counterpart of the wise old man, see earth mother below.

Dream Two

In April 2000, a dream dealt with a constant reoccurring nightmarish theme—a loss of control and feeling overwhelmed by my unconscious. "NBA basketball player Mike Jordan denies his extravagant and out-of-control gambling problem. The public expresses concern over his denial."

Interpretation: Jordan represented my shadow archetype—my blind spots, inferiorities, and denied potentialities. Through gambling (my irresponsibility), I was throwing away my dream of writing. The poker chips symbolized the circular child archetype. I was losing the opportunity to find healing, light, and self-realization. I was in a psychological state of severe denial, the same state a gambler is in when he or she gives way to addiction. The shadow archetype is always the same gender as the dreamer.

So my unconscious called for my attention to return to my dream of writing. But because of my repression, resistance, anxiety, and fear, I failed to objectively self-analyze my dreams or emotional condition. Jung (1985) explained that, if we resist the dream and self-change, the unconscious only becomes a terrifying threat, as occurred for Scrooge.

Dream Three

In late September 2000, unbeknownst to me at this time, I had a portentous dream that reflected that a change and a new dawn loomed near. I wrote, "I had to cross a huge intricate Ferris wheel-like contraption, which was a difficult and complex task. Yet I felt determination and strength in the effort. I had to continually cross the edifice until I had mastered and completed it."

Interpretation: The circular Ferris wheel represented self-healing, the totality of the self, the vortex of the unconscious, and the wheel or clock of time and death. The repeated crossing of the edifice represented my journey across the threshold into the unconscious to seek and find. The dream was prescient and compelled me to move toward my future work. Jung (Jung et al. 1968, 66) maintained that dreams can have this portentous dimension.

Dream Four

In late October 2000, I had a dream that seemed like a *big dream*. "I am standing in front of St. Felicitas School—the elementary school that I attended. I am standing in an intense thunderstorm with powerful lightning. I am a storm watcher or storm harmonizer. I stand facing northward, and I watch storms and measure the lightning voltage. My right arm extends up toward the sky, and lightning bolts constantly blast electrifying power through my arm and body. I am not fearless, but rather fear with courage and strength."

Interpretation: The school represents learning, knowledge, and teaching. My gift and dharma (duty or life purpose) abides in crossing the threshold of the turmoil of adolescence and the subterranean underworld of the unconscious. For in this dark realm—the unconscious, emotions, the sea of storms—abides knowledge, power, and light. To my right stands a gymnasium, which in the past was the church where I was baptized, and thus my life purpose subsists in this work.

This dream also stood prescient for the future. Jung (1990a, 295) believed that lightning symbolizes a powerful change of consciousness. Campbell (2004, 96) wrote that Jung defined a *big dream* as a "kind of dream, where you find yourself facing a problem that's not specific to your peculiar life or social or age situation. Rather, you've run up against one of the great problems of man."

Dream Five

In February 2001 I dreamt, "There stand two dual, conscious-type males—director/actor Woody Allen and actor/comedian Jerry Lewis, who liked to explore caves. They each have a dual side. Allen, the artist, is often a neurotic, and Lewis, the comedian, is also a compassionate fundraiser for cerebral palsy. They represent my shadow and my inner conflict of conscious and unconscious imbalance. Allen and Lewis must fight to the death against actress Sigourney Weaver, who wields a vicious knife-sword with razors—like a lightning bolt—in her right hand. Weaver expresses anger because she does not get the respect from Allen and Lewis that she deserves. Weaver represents my anima archetype and stands as the quintessential female warrior/Amazon because she reflects my ideal female. She played the role of the heroine Ellen Ripley in the films *Alien* and *Aliens*. Ripley personified a balanced and radiant conscious femininity with a strong, intelligent, noncastrating masculine unconscious. This anima figure evokes a new idea or concept to me because I do not usually see the anima as a warrior, but she emanates extreme power.

Interpretation: Many messages existed in this dream. My conscious side did not take seriously the demands of my anima (Sigourney Weaver). I'd had sleep problems for weeks, and now I sensed she had been keeping me up at night. I was probably viewing, albeit unconsciously, the potentiality of the anima as a joke. The dream depicted accurately my skepticism that my anima was weak. Also, the shape of the sword in the hands of the anima was similar to the "lightning bolt" from dream four. The anima conveyed the message that, only by being in accord with the anima (the internal feminine and a balanced masculinity), could I or any male be liberated from castration anxieties and fears (feelings of impotency, powerlessness, insecurity, and inferiority). She carries the sword in her *right* hand, which denotes consciousness while the *left* implies the unconscious. My neurotic side (Woody Allen) would be severely challenged, since I liked to explore the caves (Jerry Lewis) or the unconscious.

This dream predicted my future journey and exploration of the unconscious. Jung (1990a, 135) noted that the cave abides as the place of rebirth, and Campbell (in Patillo and Manchi 1988) opined that caves lurked as the abode for male initiation rites.

When I first had this dream I did not realize its importance. The dream provided me *clues* to find what I sought. Jung (1985, 15) opined that the anima usually appears only when a conflict in the unconscious is beginning. My anima, Sigourney Weaver, portentously warned me that my descent to explore the unconscious would be a serious and dangerous endeavor. She reminded me that the anima is an indispensable weapon for power and, without the weapons, my journey could be fatal. The lightning bolt symbolizes "illumination and change of consciousness," and thus the anima/animus—the unconscious—is a source of illumination. Swords, knives, and pistols often reflect phallic symbols, and I deeply sense the sword-lightning bolt was a disguised clue that represents a phallic symbol too. Jung (157) wrote, "The phallus always means the creative mana [intuitive powers], the power of healing and fertility, the 'extraordinary' potent." Thus, overidentifying with my conscious masculine side would be a form of self-castration, and I would be "cut off" from access to the powers and healing from my anima. My anima shouts a warning to me about this dynamic. It proves indispensable to have masculine-consciousness and feminine-unconscious balance; the inverse holds true for females. Jung's (1990a, 31) comment about the anima appears to be applicable to my dream. "Behind her cruel sporting with human fate there lies something like a hidden purpose which seems to reflect superior knowledge of life's laws. It is just the most unexpected, the most terrifyingly chaotic things which reveal a deeper meaning." Furthermore, this dream reflects an example of Dr. Freud's (1998, 315) concept of dream *condensation*, where the meaning or latent content usually abides layered in the compressed structures of the dream. Freud (365) suggests that, to decipher the dream, the dreamer should focus on its most *intense* and *vivid* aspects.

Dream Six

In September 2003, I dreamt, "NBA basketball player Kobe Bryant attempts to teach basketball, but he plays out of control on the court. A black female, a master ball handler and dribbler, dominates the court. The skin of her face shines with a golden olive and blackish texture, and she has wavy, gold-blonde hair that is braided and shaped like a royal crown. The rounded braids form golden serpents that shape into the crown."

Interpretation: Kobe represents my shadow, and the black female symbolizes my anima. I can't be in harmony with myself or others if I only function with male consciousness. I must also be in accord with the internal feminine. It is the anima, the internal feminine, who has the powers to harness the potentialities and dynamism of the unconscious—serpents. The circular basketball represents the totality of me, and in order to become whole and healed, I must embrace the internal feminine/anima that is the means to healing the wounded child in me. The serpents symbolize wisdom, light, healing, and resurrection (Jung 1978, 245); their circular form represents a unity of consciousness with the unconscious. I was beginning to assimilate these unconscious potentialities for self-knowledge and self-healing. Jung suggests that the colors yellow or gold imply intuition.

Dream Archetypes and Symbols

Jung referred to archetypes as universal figures in our collective unconscious that we have inherited in our psyche. Each archetype has a different meaning or function to address the balance of the psyche, individuation process, and unrealized potentialities within. In short, Jung referred to archetypes and dream images as symbols of transformation.

- Shadow archetype—This figure always appears as the same gender as the dreamer and represents the source of one's inferiorities (Jung 1978, 8–9). The shadow reveals our infantile behaviors or attitudes that we tend to deny but need to change for our growth.
- Anima and animus archetypes—For the male dreamer, in Jungian psychology, the female figure represents the anima, the symbol and personification of the unconscious. For a woman, Jung called the male figure in her dream the animus, who represents the personification of her unconscious. Both possess a positive and negative aspect. Jung emphasized that women and men each carry an eternal image of the opposite gender inside them. Males carry the mother image and, conversely, females the father. This psychological imprint creates a projection mechanism of how we view other people, and it can color our perspectives in a positive or negative ways. Being conscious of this dynamic inside us is important because it can create conflict in relationships. When the unconscious dynamism of the anima/us becomes dominate in our attitude or behavior, early warning symptoms exist. For males, emotions of sentimentality and resentment become prevalent. Females engage in misconceptions, insinuations, and *animosity* (Jung 1978,

16). Jung (1991, 198) wrote, "The anima has an erotic, emotional character, the animus a rationalizing one. Hence most of what men say about feminine eroticism, and particularly about the emotional life of women, is largely derived from their own anima projections and distorted accordingly ... the astonishing assumptions and fantasies that women make about men come from the activity of the animus, who produces an inexhaustible supply of illogical arguments and false explanations." The function of the animus/a is to provide psychic balance for females in their feminine-consciousness and their masculine-unconscious (the inverse for males). Jung warned that one should not identify with the anima/us because doing so would create psychic imbalance and the neurosis of self-division, where one becomes a prisoner of the unconscious. Jung (1978, 16) emphasized that the animus has a positive aspect too. "Through the figure of the father, he expresses not only conventional opinion but—equally—what we call 'spirit,' philosophical or religious ideas ... the animus is a psychopomp [a guide of souls], a mediator between the conscious and the unconscious and a personification of the latter ... the animus gives to woman's consciousness a capacity for reflection, deliberation and self-knowledge."

- Wise old man archetype—Represents wisdom, knowledge, and intuition; he is a teacher, helper, and enlightener who can bring light to the dark aspects of one's life. I believe that females can experience the wise old man too, but they must sieve through the differences between the old wise man and their animus.
- Earth mother archetype—For females this archetype corresponds to the counterpart for the males, the wise old man. Jung (1990a, 186) explained that the earth mother represents a divine being as an important and powerful dynamic in a woman's unconscious. She stands for the tranquil force of nature with its natural and

instinctive powers. Mother characterizes the matrix that nourishes from the dark, deep roots of the unconscious that sprout into the life of consciousness (Jung 1985, 158–59). From years of dream work, I believe that males can experience the earth mother archetype too, but they must construe the differences between the earth mother and their anima.

- Child archetype—Jung (1990a, 159, 164) maintained that the child archetype represents the dreamer's potentiality and can be symbolized by the dreamer's daughter or son, a male or female child, or youth. This archetype is often symbolized by a circular or sphere-shaped image (164), but the child can mutate into various images such as a jewel, a pear, or a flower (160). On the one hand, Jung (160) emphasized that the child motif can represent the real yet ambiguous deep darkness of the human psyche. On the other hand, the child motif symbolizes the unity of opposites (the circle) and exists as a harbinger of healing, light, and expanded consciousness in order to triumph over darkness (164, 169). Lastly, Jung (170) wrote that the child, birthed in the womb of the unconscious, represents the inner drive toward self-realization.
- Trickster archetype—The trickster represents a figure like a clown who uses hyperbole, incongruity, the absurd, or the bizarre in order to make us face our shadows—our blind spots and inferiorities (Jung 1990a, 270).

Dream Symbols

- Water represents unconscious forces, cleansing, and healing. Water in movement connotes the energy and flow of life (Jung 1985, 13).
- Sun connotes consciousness and illumination (Jung 1990a, 379).

- Moon represents the death and rebirth cycle.
- Mandala or circle symbols denote unity and totality (Jung 1978, 31).
- Trees connote mother symbols and the impulse to life (Jung 1990b, 233).
- Animals symbolize the dynamism and instinctive aspects of the unconscious (Jung 1990a, 366).
- Dogs represent loyalty and sometimes guardians of treasure (Jung 1990b, 372).
- Cats signify anger and poor temperament (Freud 1998, 258).
- Serpents generally personify the unconsciousness (Jung 1990a, 370) and can have a positive or negative connotation. Serpents are the gargoyles that protect the sacred truths of the tree of knowledge of good and evil and are considered the guardians of treasure (Jung 1990b, 372). They represent knowledge because we fear the truth (Jung 1990a, 317). Snakes connote transformation and regeneration because they shed their skin and, hence, are the healing serpent (Jung 1976, 393). The snake signifies wisdom, light, and healing (Jung 1978, 245). On the other hand, if the serpent evokes anxiety or fear, it warns of danger because the conscious mind has been moved off its psychological center and balance (Jung 1990a, 166). Therefore, the snake can evoke the threat of being strangled by unconscious forces (Jung 1991, 125).
- Birds represent spirit symbols (Jung 1990a, 334).
- Fish symbols reflect nurture and energizing effects on the unconscious (Jung 1990a, 142) or a particular content of the unconscious (370).
- Crabs represent resurrection because, like the snake, the crab sheds its outer layer (Jung 1990a, 342).
- Houses represent the field of ego consciousness.
- Fire can represent God, the divine, love, and sexual passion. Fire, metal, or maize, natural elements,

symbolize the advancement of culture (Jung 1990a, 169).

- Color symbols—Blue indicates air, and red connotes feelings (Jung 1990a, 322). Yellow or gold imply intuition (379). Gold conveys sunlight, value, and divinity (305).
- Numbers symbols—Three is the masculine number and four the feminine (Jung 1990a, 247). Twelve equals time.
- A cross or quaternity (four points) symbol represents suffering and urges unity, redemption, wholeness, and healing (Jung 1985, 208).
- Redeemer symbols are universal archetypes that can be represented by a fish, rabbit, snake, lamb, or human figure (Jung 1985, 124).
- For an excellent online source on dream symbols, see Dream Moods' "Dream Dictionary," located at http://www.dreammoods.com/dreamdictionary/ (accessed November 10, 2011). In addition, I recommend *Man and His Symbols*, by Carl Gustav Jung, et al., as an introductory book about dreams. I particularly suggest part I, which was written by Jung. Until this book was published, Jung had refused to a write a book for the general public. But then one night he had a dream that compelled him to write this book.

Key Points

- Everyone has access to an underutilized mentor within them—the messenger of dreams, a.k.a. the wisdom of the unconscious. By analyzing your own dreams, you can access the dream messenger, and this messenger will be a reliable and perspicacious teacher and guide for your individuation and self-healing.
- Dream symbols provide clues about an adolescent or anyone's unique identity, goals, path in life, potentialities,

and pathways to obtaining psychological and emotional balance.

- The more poignant a dream, the more our dream messenger is trying to get our attention because we have failed to listen. Nightmares or dream dragons function to "open us up" if we are resistant, in denial, or repressing.

- We should embrace dream messages. Jung and Freud believed that humans have an *instinct* for self-healing. Moreover, Jung referred to the *circle* as a universal symbol for wholeness and healing (see chapter 5). The circle symbol appears often in dreams because it represents the totality of the self and healing. So our dreams compose a means to self-heal.

- Jung maintained that archetypes comprise the images of our instinctive nature; therefore, by listening to our dreams and instincts—the deep inner voice—we can harness the potentialities of the archetypes within us.

- Keep a pen and notebook next to your bed. When you recall a dream, write down as many details as possible. Include people, places, animals, shapes, colors, and anything else that comes to mind. Then write down all the emotions that the dream evoked in you since. These emotions—*latent content*—provide the clues for interpretation.

Sixteen

Self-Analysis 2: Journal Writing

Journal writing, like reading, provides a means by which we can maximize the power of the "word," which penetrates the depth of human thought, emotion, and the unconscious. Since I conversed with Carol in May 2000 (see chapter 10), I wrote daily and eventually realized the benefit of daily writing, not just for me but for anyone. Writing shifts our invisible thoughts into tangible language. Writing is a useful tool to assist adults or teens to be more attuned to themselves and to express their inner depths and increase self-understanding. Journal writing presents a way to express and release the daily thoughts, insights, family relationships and conflicts, work experiences, goals, and all the emotional baggage of the day so your mind is at peace at bedtime. Through solitude in a sacred place and dream self-analysis, your unconscious and deeper self will arise and it will likely spark moments of deep insights about yourself, relationships, your past, solution to problems, ideas for projects, and so forth. A journal is an excellent place to log these realizations.

You can write about anything that comes to your mind in a journal. You might journal about future goals or dreams, past memories, concerns or frustrations, and events of the day, and you can include emotions of hurt, anger, or joy. Writing helps you discover your emotional depths and is a complementary exercise for recapitulation (see chapter 13). Writing is not just a release mechanism for our emotional baggage from the past, it presents a more detailed and informative narrative. In short, writing helps to identify emotions with language and enhances one's ability to objectively self-evaluate his or her life.

In the 1980s, I worked at Mercy Home for Boys & Girls in Chicago. As part of the treatment program for midadolescents, Dr. David Patrick, the director and a psychologist, mandated that each youth write an autobiography of the presenting problem (e.g., family conflict, sexual or physical abuse, committing sexual or physical abuse, parent abandonment or neglect, or running away) that led to their temporary placement in the program. In short, each youth had to identify his or her problem and take responsibility to make the necessary psychological and behavioral changes. Identifying and admitting the problem is the huge first step toward self-change or any conflict resolution. Dr. Patrick had an admission requirement of a baseline IQ of around 90 because of the emphasis on daily group therapy and a written autobiography; therefore, journal writing requires an average intelligence to participate in this task. I recommend journal writing as a means of assisting individuals to not just identify problems and goals but to release pent up emotions, thoughts, frustrations, wishes, and so on.

Journal writing helps teens or adult stay centered and creates "movement" in their lives toward independence, future goals, and personal growth. I prefer to combine my dream work and writing journal in one notebook for convenience. And actually, both relate to each other. Connections often occur between the two since dreams often relate to our activities from the previous day.

Just like solitude in a sacred place, writing requires spending time with oneself. Start slow and write for five to fifteen minutes a day or even just a few days a week if your time is limited. Make journal writing fun and it will be an activity of great importance— self-exploration. Write about anything that presses upon your mind—daily activities, moods, concerns, future goals, relationships, school, work, experiences from childhood, and so forth. Personally, I usually write about my present concerns and emotions, particularly when something seems to be pressing on my mind, or I like to log spontaneous insights about the psychology of other people or myself. Also, when my shadow, bratty behaviors, or frustrations arise, I like to identify and elaborate on them and note how I need to change.

Reviewing your journal after an incubation period of a few weeks or months is a good practice that can enhance your objective self-analysis. Like exercise or recapitulation, writing can give one a jolt of release, and thereby, over time it brings a sense of increased clarity about one's life, goals, and self-identity.

Yet, just as with any endeavor you undertake, you will find that you're more proficient than others. The occasional writers' block often means you have a sense of uncertainty in the focus and direction of writing. Simply writing about anything will help to work through this common obstacle.

A note of caution: if writing on any subjects evokes feelings of poignant anxiety, melancholy, or anger that lingers and bleeds into other aspects of your life for days or weeks, you might need a professional guide, perhaps a psychotherapist, to explore these deeper issues. If your teenager starts a journal, you should observe him or her to see if any drastic or melancholic emotional changes take place. Despite natural curiosity, I do not recommend reading a teen's or anyone's journal unless they give permission. I suggest maintaining privacy for anyone's journal unless the adult or teen wants to share the material. Even if your teenager might be struggling in life with melancholy or something, maintaining personal boundaries and respecting the confidentiality of the document is important. Anytime you need to address emotional concerns, do so through direct communication as recommended in chapter 10.

Writing, whether in a journal or as part of psychological treatment, compares to literature writing because, in literature, the author is telling the story of fictional characters, while in journal writing the author is telling his or her own story. We all have a human story that is both connected to and unique from all other stories—both fictional and nonfictional; however, journal writing is an extremely personal task and "sacred" like the activity of solitude. We can share our stories with others but with this cautionary note:

years ago, a clinical supervisor of mine conveyed a caveat about "self-disclosure" from a psychotherapist to a client. The psychologist emphasized that the therapist should only reveal his or her personal life *if the story is related to the client's problem and the story will help move the client forward in his or her treatment and personal growth.* Therefore, I suggest this prudent proviso be followed whether in journal writing or in caregivers' communication with children.

Adolescents and adults need to be the authors of their story in life so they will take responsibility and independently develop the plot of their lives. As Campbell emphasized (see chapter 10) the universal heroic deed, which I believe stands as the essence of the call of adolescence, abides in the quest to discover our unique potentialities within us. So journal writing provides an additional means to discover our inner emotional depths.

In this chapter, I will share some of my experiences and realizations from journal writing and how the practice helped me come to terms with aspects of my past and move toward increased self-healing, resolution, and self-realization.

Self-Discovery and Release

In May 2000, I began journal writing in earnest, and I realized that the assault of anxiety and nightmares from my unconscious related to my resistance to following through on my inner dream to write a book on adolescence. I wrote on various topics such as my childhood experiences as my friend Jake had counseled (see chapter 10). I explored my *shadow* of self-doubt about writing a book. Sometimes I thought, *Oh, I can't do that. I am not smart enough. Who am I to write a book on adolescence?* As Campbell (in Patillo and Manchi 1988) revealed, the dragon is the embodiment of *self-doubt*, and we must face the dragon (see chapter 11). Although the dragon symbolizes greed, it refers to a sense of "holding on" to something that obstructs our growth, individuation, and unrealized potential.

As I recorded and explored my ambivalence and self-doubts, I inevitably confronted a deep, secret wound that had inflicted me in first grade during my hospitalization as king of the fakers. I failed first grade, and that had left a piercing wound of self-doubt and presumed intellectual inferiority within me. Yet as I wrote, I suddenly recalled the reason I did not like school and faked polio. For weeks or months after school, an older, male bully would grab the jacket of my right shoulder and walk me three blocks to the corner of my home. I hated school. I felt intimidated, insecure, unprotected, and powerless. I felt ashamed to tell my parents because I was sure a nun had told this older boy to walk me home.

A short time before the bully had started taking me home, I'd walked out of St. Felicitas School with a classmate. We chatted merrily—I distinctly remembered that I felt happy as a lark. While we walked and conversed, I naturally became slightly distracted, given that I was engrossed in conversation. As we approached the corner of 84th Street and Blackstone Avenue, where a patrol boy stood on duty, I took a single step into the street, but I immediately caught my mishap and stopped. Suddenly, a nun grabbed me and spanked my rump, and then she verbally scolded me for my error. She should not have done that. Although I was only five, I knew how to cross a street. Heck, Mom and Dad did not have time to hold my hand to cross the street. I had to learn a degree of age appropriate autonomy because I had four younger siblings in a family of eight. I think the nun instructed this older boy to take me home, and she erred there too because nobody should ever give a child power over another child. Maybe she was having one of those "bad days" and discharged her anger and frustration on me.

At age fourteen when I physically grew and possessed the confidence to fight if necessary, I walked to the bully's house and rang the doorbell. I planned to tell him how I felt about the incident and that I did not like how he'd grabbed my shoulder every day. And I thought about roughing him up some if necessary too. Fortunately, no one answered the door, and I never returned. I can become a real madman when I am defending the wounded boy within me. I am not any different from Kurt or Rafael, but their pain looms greater than mine.

Although by the time I was journaling about these events, I had earned two master's degrees and read books voraciously for years, my feelings of intellectual inferiority still lurked deep in my psyche—my *shadow* personified by the wounded boy within. I needed to face this issue through journal writing and reflective thought and come to a resolution.

This disappointment in first grade was launched by an unforgettable moment when my mother read to me the report card's notice of failure. In this moment, I felt extreme shame, self-doubt, guilt, and inferiority. However, journal writing freed my mind to better evaluate the complete scenario more objectively. I had blamed myself, and now I experienced a sense of release, a cathartic purge, which enabled me to objectively face up to my past. I had the liberating realization that it was not my fault that I'd failed first grade. As I wrote and discharged my emotions into a story, the words transmuted into a more transparent, concrete reality because the writing process provides a clearer picture, similar to both the process of writing a manuscript where, in the writing itself, the subject matter or storyline comes alive and the use of autobiographical writing for therapy as applied by Dr. David Patrick. My experience holds that journal writing will help the writer better see and understand him or herself.

In other areas of my life, writing helped me to decrease and eventually eliminate the anxiety and depression that had plagued me because I had created *movement* toward my dream to write. I wrote about painful childhood experiences such as my faking acts, bed-wetting, and the struggles of puberty. Doing so not only provided an emotional release and increased my self-understanding, it produced useful material for this book. In addition, writing about my past helped me realize the huge influences of three men in my life, my football coaches from grammar and high school. They stood as powerful role models for me because all three exhibited a balanced and strong manhood since. Each had a firm, strong, disciplined demeanor, yet each possessed human compassion.

Through journal writing I rediscovered the peak experiences of my boyhood, such as when my father taught me to ride a bike and to swim, as well as the influential teachers, classes, and books that affected me. Through journal writing one can discover people who had huge influences in their lives, such as teachers, aunts or uncles, and so forth. The experiences of lives help define who we are as individuals. The discoveries we make through writing can broaden our self-perspective, and we can appreciate positive past experiences.

But for many of us, writing about and facing the past can create anxiety and avoidance, which is a natural reaction. The sagacious shaman Don Juan Matus maintained that, to become a woman or man of knowledge, one needs to erase his or her personal history (Castaneda 1991b, 9–17). He did not mean that one should deny him or her. Rather we should embrace the intention of letting it go so we can overcome the human tendency to *indulge* in the past, which becomes an obstruction to the pursuit of self-knowledge. The technique of recapitulation (see chapter 13) assists this process, and journal writing is an additional means by which we can obtain more specific information and come to terms objectively with the past. It also aids our ability to let it go.

Finally I realized that I was not at fault for failing first grade, so I forgave and let it go of my self-doubts about my intellectual abilities. By identifying my feeling of inferiority and the experience that had been the foundation of this feeling, I placed the experience in perspective and used it to become stronger, more intelligent, insightful, and knowledgeable of my unconscious and self. Therefore, through writing, I engaged in a self-imposed rite of purification to cleanse the internal wounds of childhood. Jung (1991, 169–70) wrote, "For in every adult there lurks a child—an eternal child, something that is always becoming, is never completed, and calls for unceasing care, attention, and education." The wounded child within us manifests in our shadow, and as Jung (1978, 8–9) wrote, it composes the source of our inferiorities. Other theorists discuss this angry, wounded "child ego state" that arises in us (see Berne 1973; Sarno 1998).

So my dragon was the embodiment of my feeling of failure when I didn't pass first grade and of the wounded and angry boy within me. By the same token, the dragon consisted of my "holding on" to self-protective behaviors and the false belief of intellectual inferiority.

Indeed, I had encased myself in a psychologically rigid and self-protective fortress to protect the hurt boy within me. Consequently, I avoided the *risk* and challenge of act on the high adventure and seeking my inner dormant potentiality to write; therefore, the dragon had to open me up.

I needed to confront the scourge of intellectual inferiority, and journal writing helped me do this and to identify other unconscious problems and to purge these internal wounds. Over time, I discovered a newfound self-confidence in the art of writing. I ascertained that, like Marcus and the children of darkness, I too experienced the triadic scourge of inferiority—anxiety, fear, and aggressive self-destruction. So I overcame this false belief of inferiority as the educator Paulo Freire (1970) recommended via *action and self-conquest*—through journal writing and reflective thought in my sacred place. Thus, I *ejected this image of inferiority* and failure, which marked the beginnings of an internal revolution. By ejecting this image I gave myself a magical "memory charm," where the painful memory did not get erased but, rather, the false belief vanished (also see recapitulation in chapter 13). Furthermore, this act of ejection was like a burial rite at a funeral, but in this self-imposed ceremony I identified, grieved, and let go of the wounds of my childhood. Finally, Jung (1977, 184) summed that the purpose and driving force of the unconscious appears to be the yearning for self-realization. Although writing enabled me to perform this purge, years later I discovered the similar technique of "recapitulation" (see chapter 13). I believe that recapitulation is a superior technique because of its simple efficiency and the seemingly mysterious magical effect of breathing. Nevertheless, journal writing amplifies the thoroughness of recapitulation. So journal writing is part of the psychological, emotional, spiritual armor, along with a sacred place, recapitulation, and dream analysis.

In June 2000, after rereading psychology books and further exploration of my unconscious, anxieties, and fears, I wrote in my journal, "In the works of psychologists William Glasser (*Reality Therapy*) and Albert Ellis (*Rational-Emotive Therapy*), the two men ascertained that we create our neuroses because we don't want to take responsibility or hold false beliefs about ourselves. I am responsible for creating all this turmoil of anxiety and fear. As Jung (1977, 20) wrote, neurosis is self-division; thus I have been in internal contradiction with myself—out of balance."

I know the hard work involved in self-change and, therefore, I neither expect nor advocate that anyone follow the time-consuming path that I devoted to increasing self-realization. However, my intention since 2002 has centered on finding *shortcuts* in this process toward self-awareness, independence, and self-healing so individuals don't have to experience an emotional upheaval in their life in order to awaken to the call of change and growth. From my experience, I maintain that the four cornerstones of self-change in order of priority are a sacred place, recapitulation, self-dream analysis, and journal writing. In this time-strapped world of work and family, time is a premium. Simply beginning with the *intention* of self-realization by spending five minutes a day in a sacred place and placing a dream and/or writing journal next to your bed is a huge first step. This small step will create movement toward possible vast changes in your personal growth and sense of fulfillment.

Key Points

- Writing is a useful instrument that can assist both adults and teens to be more attuned to themselves, to express their inner depths, and to increase self-understanding.
- Write about anything in a journal. List goals; recall your past; talk about emotions of hurt, anger, or joy; get out frustrations or concerns; and record the events of the day. Writing helps you discover your emotional depths, memories, and goals and provides a means for a cathartic purge.
- Just like solitude in a sacred place, writing is an activity you do with yourself. Start slowly and write for five to fifteen minutes a day or even just a few days a week. Make it a fun activity and embrace its ability to help you explore yourself.

- Our neuroses or problem behaviors usually stem from some experience. Journal writing helps to identify, clarify, and purge internal wounds. We can then paradoxically use these dark experiences to become stronger, more intelligent, more insightful, and knowledgeable of our unconscious minds.

- Overcome false beliefs, such as feelings of inferiority by the *actions of self-conquest* like journal writing and reflective thought. Through these actions, you will gain the ability to *eject the image of inferiority* and failure.

- We often create our neuroses, such as anxiety, fear, and melancholy, because we don't want to take responsibility for some aspect of our life.

- The four cornerstones for self-change in order of priority are spending time in a sacred place, recapitulation, self-dream analysis, and journal writing. Begin simply. Set the *intention* of working toward self-discovery. Spend a few minutes a day in a sacred place, and place a dream journal next to your bed. This small step will create movement toward the likelihood of enormous changes, profound insight, and a sense of fulfillment.

Seventeen

Self-Analysis 3: Understanding the Death Instinct

This final chapter will focus on the inner dynamic of the death instinct because I sense that it is the crux of what we fear in ourselves and in others, as discussed in chapters 1, 5, and 14. Furthermore, I believe the death instinct rests as a crucial instinctive clue for self-analysis and self-healing. Like chapter 14, "Awareness of the Death Instinct," the intent of this section is to help parents and educators become more aware of the death instinct's ubiquitous presence in our lives and how we can embrace it as a messenger from the unconscious.

Freud defined the death instinct as human nature's instinctive urge to return to an inorganic state. In a similar vein, Fromm (1964, 97) described three types of regressive personality types—the sociopathic, which orients toward the "love of death and destruction" (see chapter 5); the narcissist (see chapter 12), with its fixed orientation and preoccupation with the self; and the *symbiotic*, which orientates toward the quasi-incestuous wish—not necessarily sexual—to return to the symbiotic abode of a womb-like, carefree state of security, nurture, and unconditional love in order to escape a life without anxiety, fear, conflict, responsibility, and independence. This internal tour de force or wish to return to the *wholeness* experienced in the womb is a powerful influence in our lives as we undertake the ongoing struggle against dependency in all its variant forms. Fromm (1964, 113) called these regressive behaviors the *syndrome of decay*. Although violence and suicide are extreme manifestations of the death instinct gone amok, as is a sociopathic personality, behaviors of dependency are subtly self-destructive. This wish to return to the womb manifests in a wide range of elusive behaviors that we should be aware of for self-analysis and in our evaluation of adolescents or students, such as

- when an individual who is age eighteen or over has no ambition or goals, still lives at home with his or her parents, and neither attends school nor has a job;
- when a youth or young adult clings to the chains of dependency in the criminal justice system through needed supervision of probation or parole officers, thus ensuring he or she is at risk of returning to the cultural substitute for the womb—prison.

These behaviors indicate a state of dependent, entropic self-deterioration, in contrast to a journey (the call and adventure of adolescence) toward self-discovery and independence. Fromm (1964, 113) labeled this conflict the *syndrome of growth versus the syndrome of decay*. These behaviors mark the beginnings of the syndrome of decay (a slow death of one's potential self) and, like signs of suicide ideation, signal a warning. They are symptoms that the balance is teetering and the self-destructive force within—the death instinct—may be dominating and may overwhelm the self. If that happens, self-destructive behaviors, whether projected outwardly into criminality and violence or internalized into depression and suicide, will result. Thus, we can analyze ourselves, a son or daughter, students, and society through the window of the "behaviors of growth versus behaviors of decay." While the self-destructive behaviors are symptoms of decay, I believe, they can be, albeit paradoxically, construed as instinctive yet ineffective attempts for self-healing—*wholeness* (see chapter 5).

The dependency behaviors of decay should be analyzed, like suicide ideation, *metaphorically* as a truism of life, humanity, and culture; that is, *something needs to die* or, simply, the person needs "to separate from" or "let go" of something. Perhaps, on the microcosm level, it is their hold on childhood and dependency on parents, pain of past relationships, whether a marital divorce or the end of a romance, personal failure, sexual or physical abuse, loss and abandonment of parent/s. However, on the macrocosm level, what needs to die might be something *cultural*, as in the case of Romeo and Juliet; their deaths represented symbolically that which needed to die—not them, but the anachronistic form of arranged marriage that denied the spontaneity and bliss of romantic love. Remember that death and rebirth implicitly incorporate the cycle of life, just as adolescence marks the *death* of childhood and the *birth* into adulthood. So behaviors of decay can be understood and interpreted symbolically, just like the symbols in dreams. Jung et al (1968, 41) maintained that symbols are meaningful whether in a dream symbol or with behavior.

In China (23 percent) and South Korea (20 percent), a high percentage of high school students experience suicidal ideation. Why? I maintain that the immense pressure students experience around academic examinations is the source of this heartache and stress. In an article entitled "Exams in South Korea: The One-Shot Society," *The Economist* explained that a single exam determines whether or not a student is accepted into the best universities (*The Economist*, December 17, 2011, 54–56). Thus the students' future educational and professional careers are at risk. If students fail to make the grade, then they and parents might feel shame and lose face. Consequently, sometimes in Asia, the "only way" to save face becomes suicide. Therefore, the primary problem rests not with teens but with an anachronistic educational testing system that puts enormous pressure on students.

However, I believe this norm of "saving face" by suicide suggests a deeper obstacle in the adolescent psyche. I sense "saving face" has a dual Janis-faced aspect with positive and negative sociocultural consequences. On the one hand, saving face in social interactions (a social norm that curtails aggression) creates the upside of social harmony and order in the East—far greater than in most Western countries. For example, I have observed Filipino's who will make every effort not to give offense to anyone in order to avoid conflict and a possible aggressive response from someone who "lost face." On the other hand, I maintain that "saving face" is a cultural defense mechanism that shields the universal scourge of *inferiority* of individuals; as a result, I believe that Asian youth communicate metaphorically another compulsory and unfulfilled human need through suicide. In the East, cultures emphasize that one's social role is his or her sole identity and life purpose (Campbell in Patillo and Manchi 1988; 2004, 103–4; 1988, 68–9); therefore, I sense suicide for these youth conveys an unconscious yearning to break free—a "death"—from the chains of a restricted social identity and to experience a "rebirth" of their unique individuality and unrealized potentialities. I have encountered Asians in the Philippines, Singapore, and Thailand who established a "balanced" self with their unique individuality and with their social roles. Besides their bilingualism, they have one thing in common—avid reading of both Western and Eastern literature. I maintain that, through reading Western literature, they were able to "identify" with fictional or nonfictional "individual" characters, which enhanced their own unique human development and identity formation. In addition, these acquaintances did not live in cultures that promoted a zealous nationalism that projects national *superiority*, which functions as a compensatory defense against *inferiority*. This suicidal phenomenon is, then, a political and cultural problem as well, though authorities would probably retort that the one-shot test system is part of the tradition, culture, and belief system.

Therefore, the suicidal ideation of youth is a symptom that likely masks deeper sociocultural problems. The behavior of a society's youth resounds like an oracle from the unconscious to warn individuals and society of cultural imbalance that needs remedy.

In contrast, in the United States, a Western culture based on individualism, I sense that adolescent behavior manifests differently but with a similar beacon of warning. Recall that, in chapter 3, we looked at research that suggested the West is a depressive culture and examined the implicit relationship between depression and aggression (Storr 1970, 80). I think that suicide, and particularly the slew of mass murders/suicides at schools since the 1990s, rings a dire message—for these youth, society seems to have failed to provide a means for young people to move toward a strengthened manhood. I sense the gruesome behavior of these "misanthropic" youths is a warning to the collective society that we need a change, just like the message from a nightmarish dream warns that an individual needs to change. And the more one represses and denies the message, the more even worse nightmares follow. The violent suicidal youth nonverbally, horrifically, and unconsciously act out the actual function of a rite of passage—a psychological *death and rebirth*—but their attempts fail tragically.

My sense is that what needs to die or change is twofold:

1. On the microcosm level, since our culture does not possess standardized rites of passage for adolescents, we need to incorporate formal and informal rites that assist youth to psychologically move successfully through adolescence and into adulthood, such as those suggested in chapter 1.

   Other countries incorporate indirect and possibly unintended quasi-structural rites of passage that we should consider. For example, in Israel, at age eighteen females and males join the army for three years. After military service, traditionally the young adults travel around the world for a year or more, and upon completion of their travels, they usually enroll in university. As a result, now at age twenty-two to twenty-three (late adolescence), they are more mature and prepared to study for a career. I have met many

Israelis in my travels and during my six-week visit to Israel in 1978, and young adults clearly display a more mature, confident, secure, and balanced womanhood/ femininity and manhood/masculinity than most of their counterparts in the United States. Moreover, I believe this tradition of travel also functions as a quasi ritual of purification for the soldier's reintegration into society from the complex and stressful psychological and emotional consequences of combat. Traveling and experiencing diverse peoples and cultures provides former combatants a necessary process of detachment, impartial perspective, and resocialization. Joseph Campbell's intriguing commentary (Campbell 1988a, 234–238) on *The Odyssey* maintains that the gods' purpose for the adventures, trials, and tribulations upon Odysseus—the tenacious warrior returning home from the Trojan war—intended to rehumanize him because he was not psychologically fit to reenter society since he had been tortured with lashes, killed many Trojans with his spear (Homer 1937, 49), and abducted the wives of Trojans for his soldiers' personal use (Campbell 1988a, 234). As a result of Odysseus' sojourns, tests, and ordeals, he spent most of his time in solitude by the seashore where he mourned and wept (Homer 1937, 63). In short, during combat often the death instinct becomes the primary *modus operandi* that now must be comprehended, purged, tamed, honed, and rebalanced in the human psyche (see chapter 14).

In Mexico and the Philippines, high school ends at age sixteen. (In June 2012, the Philippines adopted the longer high school model as in the United States.) Here too, I have observed a quicker maturing process in adolescents because there exists a socioeducational structure to conclude adolescence properly—a quasi rite of passage. In Mexico, I discovered that, after high school, adolescents can enroll in a two-year preparatory school, similar to a junior college, to study nursing, education, mechanics, and better prepare them for university. This early exit from high school at age sixteen triggers a huge psychological break from adolescence and compels the youth to think and behave more maturely and seriously about career and so forth. I present these examples to better assist readers to reevaluate our culture and to spark their imagination so they might create novel ways to incorporate informal rites of passage with their children or students.

2. On the macrocosm level, I sense what needs to change deals with the *imbalanced* excesses of the economic and technological consumer culture that often ensnares youth further into psychological dependency and a superficiality of self-identity. First, evidence clearly shows that with *excessive* computer usage, youth get trapped in the dependency of the digital world of cyberspace, as evidenced with the rise of Internet addiction boot camps in places like Arizona, South Korea, and China. Clear evidence also demonstrates that excessive computer use and multitasking negatively effects cognitive and attention abilities. A Frontline documentary, *Digital Nation*, which aired on February 2, 2010, addressed this issue (Dretzin and Rushkoff 2010).

In a 1998 interview with Casey Walker, author Joseph Chilton Pearce explained that a comparative, twenty-year study from the Tubingen University in Germany revealed that teens in the mid-1990s had lost 20 percent of their sensory awareness of the environment around them as compared to a group studied twenty years earlier (Walker 1998). This unintended, deleterious effect of technology becomes further compounded by the fact that adolescents are the primary target group of consumer advertising companies. A Frontline documentary, *The Merchants of Cool*, elaborates on this phenomenon (Goodman 2001).

It appears that economic society has evolved to the point of being too *imbalanced*, and therefore, young consumers can become slowly and insidiously ensnared and *dependent* on the consumer culture. Fromm (1997) coined a term for his sociopsychological dilemma in the title of his book *To Have or to Be*. That is, excessive consumer culture allows people to orient their characters toward and find a sense of meaning through the accumulation of consumer goods (to have) rather than orienting toward and focusing on segmenting their individual capacity to love and create (to be). Fromm's succinct societal analysis can be viewed in a 1958 interview with reporter Mike Wallace (Wallace and Fromm 1958). Adverse consequences result from this *imbalance* and excessive economic and technological consumerism. First, the danger lurks increasingly in the near future that individuals will be able to choose virtual reality over reality, and I don't think that bodes well for humanity. We must ask the question, is the technology controlling humanity or is humanity controlling the technology?

First, I suggest limiting *personal* computer time to two hours maximum a day. For children ages sixteen and under, the limit should be only an hour a day, as the brain structures of these young people are not yet fully developed. Teens need to fully develop their creative and imaginative thought processes and not allow the computer to function as a proxy for this unique human craft and gift.

Second, I suggest teaching children to be "responsible consumers" and self-aware of the insidious negative effects of excessive economic consumerism. A responsible and balanced consumerism consists of (1) placing a percentage of one's salary into a savings account or investment; (2) avoiding debt such as with credit cards; and (3) living modestly by not purchasing items beyond one's essential needs for clothing, merchandise, and technological devices. The danger lurks of becoming imbalanced, overidentifying as a consumer, and being coaxed into thinking that one's identity actually consists of the social role or mask of a consumer lurks. An individual might identify with the luring images of designer fashion clothing. As noted in chapters 10 and 12, one should not overidentify with a social role or mask—which Jung called the *persona*—because it masks the genuine potential self within. This overidentification with one's social mask further impedes youth from looking inwardly to increase self-awareness; as a result, young people become cut off from their internal source of authentic power and identity—their inner emotions, instincts, and the unconscious (see chapters 3 and 12). If people do not properly experience and understand their emotional and instinctive nature, they are in danger of developing a human machinelike personality (Campbell in Patillo and Manchi 1988) without a unique sense of originality, imagination, creativity, and human compassion with the capacity to love. They will not fully understand emotions such as anxiety, compassion, fear, joy, and anger and, consequently, will fear and repress these emotions (see chapters 1, 5, and 12). Such fear and repression can become an unconscious reservoir for potential rage and violence.

These economic and technological issues are complex political and economic policy issues, but as parents and educators, being aware of this dynamic allows us to simply focus on providing a balance for children and adolescents in this economic and technological environment.

An Internal Ally: the Death Instinct

The above analysis aims to present a way for us to face the powerful mechanism of the death instinct and to utilize this phenomenon as a self-analytical tool to determine what inside us needs to die or change. Moreover, the experience can make us more conscious of the subtleties of the death instinct's presence—particularly when we become angry at ourselves or others. We can consciously embrace this dark, powerful force as an ally and messenger from the unconscious. Thus, this dark, horrific messenger—the death instinct—can be the harbinger of light and a boon for our dormant potentialities. If we practice self-analysis (in a sacred place and through recapitulation, dream work, and journal writing) and take action, we can magically create light out of the darkness and conquer self-doubt, past pain, inferiority, depression, and the chains of childhood emotional dependencies. This conscious activity is like giving oneself a "memory charm" that erases the false beliefs (Ellis 1974) that make up our inner wounds. In short, we must take the independent *inward path* and heal the wounded child within, who can create such havoc in our lives. It seems that, when the wounded child becomes angry at him or herself and depressed, the child transmogrifies into the personification of the self-destroyer/ death instinct, which Freud warned was the major threat to us and to the world. But if we take the inward *hero-path* of self-analysis and experience new dimensions of self-discovery, self-healing, and self-realization, then paradoxically, the wounded child enthroned at the vortex of the dark unconscious, can become the harbinger of unrealized potentialities. And so we can be magicians of sorts and, out of the darkness, create the light of authentic power, love, creativity, and hence—an internal revolution.

The importance of self-awareness and independence as a basis for strong womanhood and manhood is the overall theme of *The Parents' and Educators' Manual of Teenage "Rebirth."* An underlying theme focuses on the necessity of understanding and facing one's pain of life, along with its concomitant—the death instinct. Yet, as presented in chapter 1, in this process of self-discovery, we inevitably and naturally come across the major obstacle of fear—the fear of self-knowledge, of our emotions and memories, and of our potential destiny. However, we learned that the essential weapons, tools, and clues that will guide us across the threshold of fear abide in our *instincts*—the deep inner voice. Those instinctive, guiding gut feelings or *somatic markers*, triggered by the limbic nervous system, communicate the wisdom of the body and the unconscious. It is this experience of actively embracing and learning from our instincts that unifies the emotional and thinking parts of the brain and moves us toward increased emotional intelligence and self-realization. We can practice this powerful internal work by spending time in a sacred place, participating in the activity of recapitulation, analyzing our dreams, and journal writing. As a result, we can encase ourselves with psychological-emotional-spiritual armor that will protect and empower us to face the inevitable psychological battles of life, whether with one's inner emotions or relationships.

In conclusion, my experience and research compel me to believe that the aggressive death instinct often surfaces when we have not healed or attended to the angry, wounded child within us. Clearly, the aggressive and/or self-destructive behaviors of Rafael, Charles, Kurt, Marcus, Liza, John, and me marked an implosion brought on by the repressed anger of the emotionally wounded child. Yet I believe that, although this tour de force of the death instinct can be dangerous, it possesses a flipside and can offer us a life-producing function if we embrace and fully understand this phenomenon. I believe that the death instinct is, paradoxically, the matrix or core instinct for self-healing (see chapters 5 and 15). Jung emphasized that instincts actually manifest in the form and essence of the archetypes (see chapter 15). That is, archetypes comprise the images of the instincts themselves in our psyche and dreams. This rings especially true with the dream symbol of the child archetype—the mutable, circular symbol that represents healing, potentiality, light, and expanded consciousness.

Therefore, my experience and belief holds that the conscious, earthly, angry, wounded child within us is the counterpart of the unconscious, eternal child archetype. We each possess within us an identity that we might call the *wounded healer*. The source of this identity is our instinctive being, and it is implicitly connected to our relationship with nature and with the divine universe. As Campbell (1973, 161) wrote, "The sufferer within us is that divine being." Finally, my experience and unbending belief maintain that, as we follow and reflect upon our instincts and dream messages and symbols as guides, we will experience not only self-healing and novel potentialities, but more importantly, we will release the sacrificial sufferer within us who waits and yearns for our heroic return and the fulfillment of our heroic deed of redemption and atonement (at-one-ment).

Book Summary of Key Points

- Chapter 1 provides vital information on adolescent psychology, information that will help parents and educators better understand adolescence. Moreover, this material offers them a strategic device to inform and prepare the pubescent youth or teen for the vast changes during adolescence.
- Change into any unknown situation often evokes anxiety and fear in us, and I believe this is the central aspect of adolescence and the core reason that some teens struggle through this period. We can better prepare pubescent youth and teens for adolescence by providing information—a kind of road map—about what they can expect and what they need to do on this journey into the unknown terrain of adolescence. In knowledge abides power, and through knowledge, youth and adults

can become victorious over this universal obstacle of *fear*.

- Movement toward independence comprises the key psychological task of early adolescence (ages twelve to fourteen). Independence means being self-sufficient in managing one's age-appropriate responsibilities, such as homework, small jobs like cutting lawns or babysitting, and spending more time with friends. Parents can set the stage for an environment of autonomy during this early phase through a ceremony such as a birthday party at age thirteen. This event would acknowledge to the youth that she or he has approached an important milestone into adolescence and mark a clear separation from childhood.

- Early adolescence is a crucial time for parents and educators. At this early stage, they have the strategic opportunity to begin informing young people about the three stages of adolescence in order to help the teen adapt and help ease his or her anxieties and fears. At this age, teens are less defensive and more receptive to this information because they have not experienced the cognitive-emotional surge of midadolescence—the great barrier.

- Some youth might experience anxiety, fear, and even mild depression with the loss (death) of childhood. We naturally desire to hold on to childhood and fear the unknown of adolescence. Adolescents must cross the threshold of fear into adolescence—a "rebirth"—with its responsibilities and move toward self-discovery and independence. The challenges of life make us grow and mature.

- Understanding the underlying psychological causes of "abnormal" behavior is important.

- Anxiety accompanies change, separation, or possible danger—an unknown—and denotes an avoidance of something.

- Middle adolescence (from age fifteen to seventeen) triggers the big bang of human development—the emergence of a second puberty, an emotional-cognitive (feeling and thinking) surge, along with biological changes in the brain structures.

- At midadolescence teens become psychologically challenged to assimilate a prism of intense human emotions (the great barrier). These include anxiety, joy, fear, love, anger, sexuality, emotional pain, insecurity, and the urge for intimacy. Emotions serve as a humanizing force and as messengers from our unconscious that communicates via instinct—our deep inner voice.

- Parents and educators can support their children and students' process of gaining independence during midadolescence by urging teens to seek employment. A job will teach a teen about responsibility and the reality of the world of work. She or he will have to learn to be accountable to a boss, coworkers, and her or himself.

- During the midadolescence years, parents should periodically review and paraphrase the general aspects of adolescent psychology from chapter 1, reminding their teens of the importance of responsibility, accountability and independence; the surge of emotions they may face; and the natural obstacle of anxiety and fear that accompanies change and self-discovery, work, career, and college. Doing so will help keep the youth focused on the future.

- Problems with a resistant, irresponsible adolescent can feel like a battlefield. But adolescent psychology offers an enormous array of psychological weaponry and leverage for parents and educators if they use the information timely, tactfully, and strategically, focusing on the objective of helping their teen become responsible and independent. In a sense, by gaining and using this "weaponry," you are informing the youth that you know their unconscious secret of inner uncertainty, dependency, and fear of independence, but that you will provide empathic support and love, along with firmness, to guide them forward.

- During the late stage of adolescence (from eighteen to twenty-three years of age), young people's psychological task is to further consolidate their social role and identity instead of retreating into isolation. The young adult should have tentative goals for a career such as college, an apprenticeship in a trade like carpentry, full-time employment, and so forth.

- When a teen turns eighteen, parents can encourage the separation from adolescence with a ceremony or celebration along with a symbolic gift.

- Fear of the self creates most psychological problems, but if we learn to listen to our inner voice of instinct, this voice will aid us to overcome fear and, thereby, increase our emotional intelligence and independence.

- In chapter 2, we look at "abnormal" behavior as a response to fear. We examine the underlying purpose or goals of acting-out and maladaptive behaviors, discovering that, often, children act out in search of attention, power, or revenge as a means of displaying their sense of inadequacy or hidden desire for self-sabotage.

- Children need love, attention, and time with their parents. Participation in daily household activities provides a means to spend time with one's parents. These activities help us in important preadolescent developmental tasks, such as identification with our parents, which provides a masculine-feminine balance respectively for each gender.

- Sometimes we create dramas and illusions such as feigned illnesses, temper tantrums, or arguments. Despite our busy work and family lives, we need to observe and understand the behavior of children, looking for clues that they may have unmet needs, anxieties, or fears.

- Psychological research displays that the mind can physically affect the body with symptoms like paralysis or phobias for some psychological advantage such as the avoidance of independence. Neurological research suggests that the brain sends messages via neurotransmitters called neuropeptides—the biochemicals of emotion—throughout our bodies. We can increase our emotional intelligence and psychological and physical health if we view the body as the "unconscious," which is consistently sending us "messages" through our emotions (gut feelings, anxieties, and fears) and sometimes with physical symptoms such as quasi paralysis or muscle pain that ultimately provide messages and admonitions about our psychological growth and the body's desire for balance and healing.

- In chapter 3, we see that behaviors like bed-wetting are adaptive behaviors. Again, the universal obstacle of fear plays a role.
- Nearly everybody possesses emotional wounds from childhood that remain difficult to face. However, if we embrace and examine painful childhood experiences such as bed-wetting, we can bring forth a healing light of self-growth and wisdom.
- Although bed-wetting can have diverse causes, it is, at its core, an act of regression; *fear* is one of the strongest forces in the negative use of retreat. A child's fears or insecurities concerning parental love or the safety of new situations can spark regressive acts like bed-wetting.
- Teach youth that they can challenge bullies nonviolently by addressing them directly and confidently, maintaining eye contact, and asking them to stop the insulting behavior.

- Providing children with life's unique aha moments (*peak experiences*)—like learning to swim or to read a book—will increase their growth and development.

- In chapter 4, we look at how realistically applying the principles of psychology at a school for "troubled youth" created a positive culture wherein students thrived in an environment of safety and nurture. Through an examination of the nuts and bolts of the foundation at Cougarville, we explore productive methods for applying these principles in the home or classroom to make parenting, education, and disciplining easier and more effective.

- Parents and educators don't need to be perfect caregivers. Rather, they need to be fair, consistent, compassionate, and firm.

- Instill a healthy culture in home or a school by stressing that children can get their needs of love and self-worth attained through Glasser's "emotional" three Rs—by taking *responsibility* for one's life and goals, by taking action toward one's goals based on the *realistic* and practical processes of everyday life, and by adhering to ethical societal values of *right* versus wrong in one's behavior and actions.

- Any caregiver or teacher can incorporate Dr. Freud's principle of "to love and to work" because it emphasizes two essentials—(1) relationship building and (2) external activities such as academic learning, athletics, theater, or a job. These two activities will establish a solid foundation for a student's growth in skills as he or she moves toward independence. "To love and to work" summarizes the principles of most psychological theories and the great religions.

- Anthropological and psychological research indicates that all social cultures produce "anxiety"; however, healthy cultures in schools and in one's home can ward off this powerful force and provide a milieu of safety and nurture.

- Psychological research shows that understanding and expressing one's aggressive feelings appropriately is important because aggression is a natural, instinctive force for preservation of the self and family; if not, aggression can transmute into depression and can get acted out in belligerent behavior toward other people. Western cultures like that of the United States are known as depressive cultures.

- After a parent imposes a disciplinary measure with his or her child, often a *teachable moment* will surface, when parent and child can discuss objectively and genuinely the circumstances of the "conflict" and resolidify their relationship. This authentic emotional interchange is called *attunement*, and it increases the child's capacity for self-awareness and empathy. Neuroscientists have shown that these attuned teachable moments can amplify the neurological structures in the child's emotional brain referred to as *pruning*.

- Psychological research shows that the aggressive drive's primary purpose is to provide individuals the ability to independently repel any threat to themselves or their families. Therefore, caregivers must demonstrate and model to children that they can confidently express aggressive feelings and, if necessary, take appropriate action to maintain a safe environment.

- Young people need to learn how to integrate their aggression in a positive way, such as asserting their independence. Otherwise, they might become dependent and helpless adults in the future.

- Chapter 5 focuses on how we adults must appropriately challenge a student's aggressive behavior in order to maintain a safe and secure school.

- Caregivers must challenge aggressive behavior to maintain a safe environment. Beneath the mask of aggression, youth are confronting issues of fear, anger, inferiority, and identity.
- Two risk factors—the lack of meaningful relationship and, most importantly, the deprivation of human love—predispose individuals to violent aggression.
- Neuroscience research shows that the amygdala is the brain's center for fear and emotional memory—the emotional brain—and with excessive stress, it can overrule the rational mind. Psychological research suggests that aggression is at its most dangerous level when it arises spontaneously.
- The staff's most effective means of avoiding violent behavior is maintaining ongoing relationships with each student. A relationship that possesses a sense of basic trust and respect can be highly beneficial in a volatile situation and can enable the de-escalation of behaviors. All staff should be aware of a potentially violent student and be ready to respond in accord with the school's crisis intervention plan.
- Aggressive situations provide an opportunity to learn more about one's own aggressive drives and how to use this powerful force constructively in the management of volatile situations. In conflict always resides the potential for learning and personal growth. Often, behind the mask of violent aggression resides an individual trapped in fear, emotional pain, and an unfulfilled longing for healing.
- Acting-out behavior can be viewed "metaphorically" as a symbolic psychological reference to one's past; traumatized individuals often develop a negative self-concept of inferiority and self-hate; consequently, they tend to act out in a pattern of self-sabotaging behaviors.

- Psychological research shows that all behaviors are adaptive, with the unconscious intent to sooth and bring self-healing. Therefore, maladaptive behaviors—like alcohol and drug abuse and acting out sexually or violently—compose our inborn instinctive attempts to self-heal.
- We often can't see our own shadows—our infantile demands and inferiorities. But we display these shadows when we encounter conflicts with others or lose our tempers. We must work to eliminate our shadows by assessing our behaviors, attitudes, and motives. Our shadow behaviors are often simply maladaptive ways for us to overprotect the wounded child within us.

- Chapter 6 displays how relationship building, literacy, and a job can prove indispensable for a "problematic" youth's human growth and development.
- Frequently, aggressive and bizarre behaviors mask feelings of inferiority and fear of responsibility and independence. They provide an alternative social role, albeit, an antisocial one.
- When parents and school staff work together toward the student's growth, responsibility, and independence, a magical dream can happen.
- Psychological research shows that effective treatment for "problematic" teens should center on movement toward responsibility and independence—the tasks of adolescence.
- With a difficult teen, use your suit of armor. Communicate about adolescent psychology consistently, stressing words like *responsibility*, *accountability*, and *independence*. Firm, fair, and consistent discipline—tough love—proves effective.
- With a difficult child, parents and educators need to work together as a united front on the student's behavioral and academic problems and goals.

- Proven effective programs for difficult teens include wilderness programs like Outward Bound and creative school programming like a half day of school and a job in a work study.

- Chapter 7 shows how, for a traumatized and abused child like Kurt, chances of a successful adolescence and adulthood improve significantly if the child has loving caregivers and early intervention from the school system. Consequently, these children can experience the healing of human love, genuine relationships, and the development of their creative potentiality.

- The vast physical and psychological changes at midadolescence provides youth with the verbal and thinking capacity to better face, understand, and work through, in psychological treatment, their problems like abuse, feelings of inferiority, or abandonment.

- To become truly free and healed from past pain of life, one needs to emotionally experience and verbally express—a cathartic purge—the emotional wounds and upsets from the past.

- Chapter 8 shows how, for "troubled" children like Marcus, fear is often the catalyst that constructs cultural beliefs of inferiority, racial superiority, and victimization.

- An individual can project his or her inner inferiorities and fears on other people, which can spark anxiety, fear, and aggressive acting out externally toward others or turned inwardly on the individual him or herself.

- The emotional wounds or pain of life generally consist of one's unconscious inferiority and self-hate. Fear tends to maintain the false cultural beliefs like racial or gender inferiority or victimization. Through the activities of introspection, self-change, and independence, one can overcome his or her fears, inferiorities, and self-hate.

- Self-change and self-knowledge comes by becoming more aware of the unacknowledged contents in one's unconscious; this may include fears, anxieties, anger, abuse, and feelings of inferiority.

- Chapter 9 shows how Marcus, Kurt, Rafael, or anyone, can release the emotional wounds of the past as exemplified by the solitary, inward hero path of the literary character of Ebenezer Scrooge who faced and purged his inner grief.

- Frightful dream figures intend to make us aware of things we tend to deny and repress; consequently, the intensity of terror from a dream relates directly to the degree of our denial and repression. Therefore, dream figures use fear to awake and teach us to heal and grow.

- Chapter 10 presents stories and information to aid parents and educators to become more aware of the symptoms, development, and possible causes of depression and suicidal ideation. Moreover, the author presents a different way to experience and interpret depression, suicidal ideation, and the unconscious as a tumultuous wake-up call to create movement toward the fulfillment of one's unrealized human potentiality. Additionally, the author provides suggestions to help parents enact suicide prevention measures.

- Nightmares can often act as precursors and messengers of unconscious problems and psychic imbalances that need our attention.

- Jung maintained that, to treat a neurosis, we must identify the task that the patient is avoiding. We usually develop neuroses in order to avoid something from our past or present that obstructs our need for personal growth, individuation, and independence.

- The *Waste Land* represents living an inauthentic life, like when we feel trapped in our social role and our lives begin to lose a sense of purpose or fulfillment. The means to free us from the *Waste Land* is to listen to our instinctive inner voice—our heart—as a guide.

- Personal crises are messages from the unconscious to awaken us from a stagnant unfulfilled life and to move us forward to discover our unique potentiality.

- Parallels exist between adolescence and midlife; we experience in these stages similar socioemotional and psychological issues, such as separation and change, dependency versus independence, and facing new frontiers with one's unique identity and sexuality.

- When families are coping with a loss from suicide, they can (1) ensure that the grieving process includes symbolic burial rites, (2) seek professional assistance if deemed necessary, (3) use journal writing, (4) read memoirs with the theme of *triumph over adversity*, and (5) participate in volunteer work.

- Four strategies for the prevention of suicide include: (1) awareness of the symptoms of depression and suicidal risk; (2) direct communication; (3) an emphasis on exercising, laughing, and crying for emotional and psychological movement; and (4) reading memoirs of people's experience with depression and suicide ideation, such as those found in chapters 10, 16, and 17.

- Chapter 11 aims to reinforce to parents and educators the importance of reading books. The chapter shows how books were powerful means of self-illumination for three twentieth-century individuals and in my life. Reading provides an essential intellectual foundation for continued growth in one's intellectual, emotional, and spiritual development.

- An internal revolution provides a necessary offensive strategy for facing our internal psychological war with anxiety, fear, emotional wounds, and a self-destructive force inside us that can trigger aggression and self-destruction.

- Reading books is a powerful resource for self-illumination and self-change and provides an essential intellectual foundation for continued growth in one's intellectual, emotional, and spiritual development.

- The path toward self-change is twofold. We must first move through trials and tribulations. Then we can achieve a transformation of consciousness, perceiving ourselves and the world anew.

- Reading to a child starting from a very early age opens the world of the child's creative imagination, an essential part of the development of the brain and cognitive processes.

- In chapter 12, we examine the importance and benefits of daily solitude in a "sacred place."

- A sacred place can be anywhere that brings your comfort. Whether reading a book in a quiet room or sitting in a place of worship, spending time in a sacred place allows you to get *centered* and shut out the demands of the world. You are able to sit in solitude and think about your dreams, goals, or God.

- If you experience anxiety or fear in quiet solitude—don't worry. You simply have explored undiscovered dimensions of your deeper self. Then you will understand what fear primarily consists of—fear of the unknown self.

- A sacred place can be a unifying force for one's family and marriage. The sacred place is the place of inner authenticity; a means of being psychologically centered; and a catalyst for becoming more aware and releasing the anxieties, fears, and anger that can contaminate the bond of conjugal love and family ties.

- Jung (1991, 53) urges parents to be consciously self-aware because, from birth, a child is psychologically merged with the psychology of their parents.
- Our shadow consists of our infantile demands and inferiorities. Solitude can furnish us with a psychological suit of arms with which we can examine and work through these shadows, thereby increasing self-awareness and personal growth.

- In chapter 13, we explore the notion of exorcising the psychological demons that haunt us.
- Michael Lomax proposed that a quasi exorcism is needed to eject the demons of race; that is, the inner socially constructed and inherited images of inferiority, which become an invisible force, voice, or monster within individuals and burden them with shame and guilt. Fear and feelings of inferiority can spark self-destructive behaviors, such as when an abused victim becomes a violent abuser. Confronting and expelling these false images or beliefs is an act of true emancipation and movement toward genuine selfhood.
- Recapitulation consists of remembering and writing the names of people and events from one's life in silent solitude. Recapitulation—like a *rite of purification*—purges the psychological and emotional baggage from our lives. One should recapitulate the most pertinent events listed until the intense emotional content has been dispelled. Deep breathing and walking help in the process of recapitulation. Recapitulation produces a profound magical effect because breathing combined with conscious *intention* puts the mind-body in accord with the powerful instinct of self-cure.
- If we truly desire to recapitulate but resist, then a breathtaking event could happen that would open us to recapitulation. The ancient shamans called this occasion *the usher*.

- The usher may come in the form of a petrifying dream messenger in nightmares, as when archetypal figures bring warnings by producing acute anxiety and fear in order to awaken and move us toward change, healing, self-realization, expanded consciousness, and personal growth—like the episode with the negative lab report.
- Jung referred to these random but meaningful incidents as *synchronicities*.

- Chapter 14 provides parents and educators with an increased awareness of the instinct of aggression within us. Individuals can harness the death instinct as an internal guide to show them what needs to change or "die" in their lives and help move them forward in their personal growth, self-healing, and independence with a sense of resurrection and rebirth.
- Freud warned that cultures need to understand and master the human aggressive instinct.
- Our aggressive drive can be used positively for self-defense, but sometimes it can deviously arise as a self-destructive force, as in a "bad day" incidence, where one mishap snowballs into a series of blunders. In such incidents, the emotional brain suddenly dominates the rational brain; however, we can reduce the charged emotions by consciously calming down with deep breathing and *reframing* logically the precipitating events. Some precursors of the death instincts presence include forgetfulness, accident proneness, irritability, anger, bad mood, abusive language, and aggression.
- Parents and educators can help teens to be more self-aware of the death instinct when *teachable moment*s surface; these moments may include media coverage of issues like personal suicide and suicidal bombers or when local teens participate in unhealthy behaviors like truancy or gang membership.

- Chapter 15 focuses on the self-analysis of one's dreams and the discovery of dream messengers as reliable and perspicacious teachers and guides for one's individuation and self-healing.
- Dream symbols provide clues for an adolescent or anyone to discover their unique identities, goals, paths in life, and potentialities and to obtain psychological and emotional balance.
- A poignant dream is the unconscious's attempt to get our attention because we have not been listening.
- We should embrace dream messages. Jung and Freud believed that humans have an *instinct* for self-healing. Moreover, Jung referred to the *circle* as a universal symbol for wholeness and healing (see chapter 5). The circle symbol appears often in dreams because it represents the totality of the self and healing. So our dreams compose a means to self-heal.
- Jung maintained that archetypes comprise the images of our instinctive nature; therefore, by listening to our dreams and instincts—the deep inner voice—we can harness the potentialities of the archetypes within us.
- Keep a pen and notebook next to your bed. When you recall a dream, write down as many details as possible. Include people, places, animals, shapes, colors, and anything else that comes to mind. Then write down all the emotions that the dream evoked in you since. These emotions—*latent content*—provide the clues for interpretation. Emotions help us understand our dreams, the deeper self, and the unconscious because they are messages from the mind-body and the unconscious to take action—*emotion*—and to acquire the wisdom from the unconscious.
- Chapter 16 focuses on the benefits of journal writing as a useful tool to assist teens or adults to be more attuned with themselves and to express their inner depths and

increase self-understanding. Write about anything in a journal, including one's emotions, concerns, and goals.

- Writing aids us in identifying emotions by putting them into language and, thereby, increases self-introspection about one's past and present life. Our neuroses or problem behaviors usually relate to our past; therefore, journal writing assists us in identifying and releasing ourselves from our emotional wounds. Frequently, we manufacture our neuroses—such as anxiety, fear, and melancholy—because we wish to avoid taking responsibility for some facet of our lives.

- Overcome false beliefs, such as feelings of inferiority, by the *actions of self-conquest* like journal writing and reflective thought; thereby, you will gain the ability to *eject the image of inferiority* and failure and begin an internal revolution.

- Solitude in a sacred place, recapitulation, self-dream analysis, and journal writing compose the four cornerstones on which self-change is built. Begin simply. Set the *intention* of working toward self-realization. Spend five minutes a day in a sacred place and place a dream journal next to your bed. These small steps will create movement toward the potentiality of vast changes, personal growth, and a sense of fulfillment.

- Chapter 17 concludes with a deeper analysis of the death instinct because it is what we fear in ourselves and others; however, paradoxically, the death instinct abides as an instinctive guide toward self-analysis and self-healing.

- *Syndrome of decay* behaviors, such as the sociopaths' zeal for death and destruction or the narcissists' fixation on the self or the symbiotic, dependent youth's wish to return to the security of the womb should be analyzed, like suicidal ideation, as a manifestation that *something needs to die* or be "let go." The "death" might be of something like a broken romance or past sexual abuse. Alternatively, what needs to die might be something in the culture at large, such as an aged precollegiate examination system that puts undue pressure on high school adolescents and leads to suicidal ideation.

- Suicidal behavior often conveys symbolically the cultural imbalances in a country that need to be remedied—that is, a place that needs the "death" of the old structures and a "rebirth" of change.

- Some countries instill quasi-structural rites of passage—such as compulsory military service for both females and males at age eighteen or when high school ends at age sixteen—that we in the West should ponder such as compulsory military service for females and males at age eighteen or when high school ends at age sixteen.

- Teach children to be responsible consumers by being aware of the potential pitfalls of the excessive use of technology and consumerism, such as personal debt.

- By understanding and embracing the death instinct as an ally and messenger, we can grasp the warnings to determine what inside us or in our society needs to die or change.

- Medical and psychological research suggests that the aggressive death instinct often manifests in the wounded, angry child within us as exemplified with the aggressive and/or self-destructive behaviors of Rafael, Charles, Kurt, Marcus, Liza, John, and me. However, the death instinct seems to be implicitly related to the human instinct of self-cure because our instincts make up the archetypes, such as the child archetype—the alterable circular dream symbol that signifies healing and potentiality—in our psyche and dreams.

- We have an identity of sorts with the divine universe as *wounded healers*. Therefore, if we contemplate our instincts and dream messages, we will encounter self-healing and unique potentialities and, most importantly, we will release the sacrificial sufferer within us.

Epilogue

Our journey into the dark, mysterious, and wonderful world of adolescence now comes to a close. I hope that you now possess a greater understanding of adolescence and psychology in order to enhance your self-knowledge, self-awareness, and independence and to enable you to boost the personal growth of your children or students. The children of darkness, such as Rafael, Charles, Marcus, Kurt, and Lisa, instilled an indelible imprint upon my memory, and I hope their stories generated knowledge and light in your lives, as they did in mine.

In a sense, adolescence never ends because the adventure of self-discovery does not cease. Sometimes, old memories or emotional wounds might resurface, but now you've acquired a means to extinguish these shadows, false beliefs, and inferiorities through the techniques of recapitulation and journal writing and as exemplified by Scrooge, Simon, and Charles. We discussed adolescent psychology as a tool to better understand and guide teens through adolescence and to increase self-knowledge. We also saw how the general maxim of love and work transformed the likes of Charles the Prince. Likewise, we addressed the importance of listening to the deep inner voice of *instinct* as a means to crossing the threshold of fear and embarking upon the hero path of self-discovery, which will lead us to a strengthened womanhood or manhood. We learned the importance of a sacred place as the matrix and central command center for self-empowerment and self-realization. In solitude, we can encase ourselves with an invisible warrior's panoply of armor with which we can face the internal and external psychological battlefields of life. In the same vein, we can analyze our dreams in order to develop greater self-understanding and experience the vast treasures and wisdom of the unconscious.

Remember that, if you encounter the pain of life, you are not alone. You implicitly possess the means to overcome the darkness because the light of potentiality lies within you. Suicidal ideation conveys a warning that something—such as a romance, the pain from the loss of loved one, memories of past abuse, or feelings of inferiority—needs to die and not the individual. If necessary, find a skilled physician of the soul in the healing art of psychotherapy to assist you. In an uncanny and extraordinary way, simply identifying what troubles us (Campbell in Patillo and Manchi 1988b) often allows us to rise from the depths of despair, as my journal writing displayed. It seems like language (the word) functions to unify the unconscious and consciousness. Remember too that your unconscious and the transcendent universe will honor your *intention* to seek the dream of your potentiality.

Finally, we learned that the techniques of solitude, recapitulation, and dream work implicitly provide a means to evoke and employ the powerful instinct of self-cure within us. If we follow and reflect upon our instincts and dream messages and symbols as guides, we will likely experience not only self-healing and novel potentialities but, more importantly, a profound sense of identification, understanding, love, meaning, and fulfillment of the divine gifts and mystery within you. So I hope that someday we will continue our conversation about the wonderful and mysterious world of adolescence and beyond.

Bibliography

Books

Adler, Alfred. 1979. *Superiority and Social Interest*. New York: W. W. Norton.

Algren, Nelson. 1949. *The Man with the Golden Arm*. New York: Seven Stories Press.

Albom, Mitch. 1997. *Tuesdays with Morrie: An Old Man, a Young Man, and Life's Greatest Lesson*. New York: Doubleday.

Aurelius, Marcus. 1990. *The Meditations*. New York: Oxford University Press.

Axline, Virginia M. 1986. *Dibs in Search of Self*. New York: Ballantine.

Barrie, J. M. 2008. *Peter Pan*. New York: Bantam Dell.

Beck, Charlotte Joko. 1989. *Everyday Zen: Love and Work*. New York: HarperCollins.

Berne, Eric. 1973. *Transactional Analysis in Psychotherapy*. New York: Ballantine.

Blos, Peter. 1966. *On Adolescence: A Psychoanalytic Interpretation*. New York: The Free Press.

Campbell, Joseph. 1973. *The Hero with a Thousand Faces*. Princeton, New Jersey: Princeton University Press.

———. 1988a. *Myths to Live By*. New York: Bantam.

———. 1989. *An Open Life: Joseph Campbell in Conversation with Michael Toms*. New York: Harper & Row.

———. 1999. *Transformations of Myth through Time*. New York City, New York: Harper Perennial.

———. 2004. *Pathways to Bliss: Mythology and Personal Transformation*. Novato, California: New World Library.

Castaneda, Carlos. 1974. *A Separate Reality: Further Conversations with Don Juan*. New York: Pocket Books.

———. 1982. *The Eagle's Gift*. New York: Simon & Schuster.

———. 1991a. *The Second Ring of Power*. New York: Washington Square Press.

———. 1991b. *Journey to Ixtlan*. New York: Washington Square Press.

———. 2000. *The Active Side of Infinity*. New York: Harper Perennial.

———. 2003. *The Art of Dreaming*. New York: Harper Perennial.

Dickens, Charles. 2009. *A Christmas Carol*. New York: Bantam.

Dinkmeyer, Don Sr., Gary D. McKay, Joyce L. McKay, and Don Dinkmeyer, Jr. 1998. *Parenting Teenagers: Systematic Training for Effective Parenting of Teens*. USA: STEP Publishers.

Dinkmeyer Don Sr., Gary D. McKay, and Don Dinkmeyer Jr. 2007. *The Parent's Handbook: Systematic Training for Effective Parenting*. USA: STEP Publishers.

Dostoevsky, Fyodor. 1981. *The Adolescent*. Translated by Andrew R. MacAndrew. New York: W. W. Norton.

Dowling, Colette. 1982. *The Cinderella Complex: Women's Hidden Fear of Independence*. New York: Simon and Schuster.

Ellis, Albert. 1974. *Humanistic Psychotherapy: The Rational-Emotive Approach*. New York: McGraw-Hill.

Erikson, Erik H. 1968. *Identity: Youth and Crisis*. New York City, New York: W. W. Norton.

———. 1978. *Childhood and Society*. New York: W. W. Norton.

Frankl, Viktor E. 1985. *Man's Search for Meaning*. New York: Simon & Schuster.

Freire, Paulo. 1970. *The Pedagogy of the Oppressed*. Translated by Myra Bergman Ramos. New York: The Seabury Press.

Freud, Sigmund. 1949. *An Outline of Psycho-Analysis*. Translated by James Strachey. New York: W. W. Norton.

———. 1952. *Dreams*. Translated by James Strachey. New York: W. W. Norton.

———. 1959a. *Inhibitions, Symptoms and Anxiety*. Translated by Alix Strachey. New York: W. W. Norton.

———. 1959b. *Group Psychology and the Analysis of the Ego*. Translated by James Strachey. New York: W. W. Norton.

———. 1962a. *Civilization and its Discontents*. Translated by James Strachey. New York and London: W. W. Norton.

———. 1962b. *The Ego and the Id*. Translated by Joan Riviere. New York: W. W. Norton.

———. 1964. *New Introductory Lectures on Psycho-Analysis*. Translated by James Strachey. New York: W. W. Norton.

———. 1998. *The Interpretation of Dreams*. Translated by James Strachey. New York: Avon.

Freud, Sigmund, and Josef Breuer. 1966. *Studies on Hysteria*. Translated by James and Alix Strachey. New York: Avon.

Fromm, Erich. 1964. *The Heart of Man: Its Genius for Good and Evil*. New York: Harper & Row.

———. 1965. *Escape from Freedom*. New York: Holt, Reinhart & Winston.

———, 1967 *The Art of Loving*. New York: Bantam.

———. 1990. *The Sane Society*. New York: Holt, Reinhart & Winston.

———. 1997. *To Have or to Be*. New York: The Continuum Publishing Co.

———. 1998. *The Art of Being*. New York: The Continuum Publishing Co.

Glasser, William. 1990. *Reality Therapy: A New Approach to Psychiatry*. New York: Harper & Row.

Golding, William. 1954. *Lord of the Flies*. New York: Penguin.

Goleman, Daniel. 1996. *Emotional Intelligence*. New York: Bantam.

Gordon, Thomas. 2000. *Parent Effectiveness Training*. New York: Three Rivers Press.

Hawking, Stephen. 1989. *A Brief History of Time: From the Big Bang to Black Holes*. London: Bantam.

Hesse, Hermann. 1997. *Siddhartha*. New York: Bantam.

Hinton, S. E. 1997. *The Outsiders*. New York: Penguin.

Homer. 1937. *The Odyssey*. Translated by W. H. D. Rouse. New York: Mentor.

Homer. 1966. *The Iliad*. Translated by W. H. D. Rouse. New York: Penguin.

Joyce, James. 1976. *A Portrait of the Artist as a Young Man*. New York: Penguin.

Jung, Carl Gustav. 1976. *The Portable Jung*. Translated by R. F. C. Hull. New York: Penguin.

———. 1977. *Two Essays on Analytical Psychology*. Translated by R. F. C. Hull. Princeton, New Jersey: Princeton University Press.

———. 1978. *Aion: Researches into the Phenomenology of the Self*. Translated by R. F. C. Hull. Princeton, New Jersey: Princeton University Press.

———. 1985. *The Practice of Psychotherapy*. Translated by R. F. C. Hull. Princeton, New Jersey: Princeton University Press.

———. 1989. *Freud and Psychoanalysis*. Translated by R. F. C. Hull. Princeton, New Jersey: Princeton University Press.

———. 1990a. *The Archetypes and the Collective Unconscious*. Translated by R. F. C. Hull. Princeton, New Jersey: Princeton University Press.

———. 1990b. *Symbols of Transformation*. Translated by R. F. C. Hull. Princeton, New Jersey: Princeton University Press.

———. 1990c. *Dreams*. Translated by R. F. C. Hull. Princeton, New Jersey: Princeton University Press.

———. 1991. *The Development of Personality: Papers on Child Psychology, Education, and Related Subjects*. Translated by R. F. C. Hull. Princeton, New Jersey: Princeton University Press.

Jung, Carl Gustave, M. L. von Franz, Joseph L. Henderson, Jolande Jacobi, and Aniela Jaffé. 1968. *Man and his Symbols*. New York: Bantam.

Kaplan, Louise J. 1984. *Adolescence: The Farewell to Childhood*. New York: Simon & Schuster.

Kesey, Ken. 1962. *One Flew Over the Cuckoo's Nest*. New York: New American Library.

Kett, Joseph, F. 1977. *Rites of Passage: Adolescence in America 1790 to the Present*. New York: Basic Books Inc. Publishers.

Knowles, John. 1975. *A Separate Peace*. New York: Bantam.

Lawrence, D. H. 1976. *Sons and Lovers*. New York: Penguin.

Lasch, Christopher. 1991. *The Culture of Narcissism: American Life in an Age of Diminishing Expectations*. New York: Norton.

Le Bon, Gustave. 2002. *The Crowd: A Study of the Popular Mind*. Mineola, New York: Dover Publications.

London, Jack. 1990. *The Call of the Wild*. New York: Doherty Associates.

———. 2001. *White Fang*. New York: Scholastic.

Lorenz, Konrad. 1969. *On Aggression*. Translated by Marjorie Kerr Wilson. New York: Bantam Books.

Ludlum, Robert. 1981. *The Bourne Identity*. New York: Random House.

Malcolm X. 1973. *The Autobiography of Malcolm X*. New York: Ballantine.

Maslow, Abraham H. 1982. *Toward a Psychology of Being*. New York: Van Nostrand Reinhold.

McCourt, Frank. 1997. *Angela's Ashes*. New York: Touchstone.

McMurtry, Larry. 1986. *Lonesome Dove*. New York: Simon & Schuster.

Naipaul, V. S. 1990. *A Turn in the South*. New York: Vintage.

New American Bible. 1987. Nashville, Tennessee: Thomas Nelson Publishers.

Nietzsche, Friedrich. 1961. *Thus Spoke Zarathustra*. Translated by R. J. Hollingdale. New York: Penguin.

———. 1990. *Beyond Good and Evil*. Translated by R. J. Hollingdale. New York: Penguin.

Peck, M. Scott. 2003. *The Road Less Travelled*. United Kingdom: Random House.

Pert, Candace B. 2003. *Molecules of Emotion*. New York: Scribner.

Prabhavanada, Swami, and Frederick Manchester, translators. 1971. *The Upanishads: Breath of the Eternal*. Hollywood, California: Vendanta Press.

Riesman, David, Nathan Glazer, and Reuel Denney. 1950. *The Lonely Crowd: A Study of the Changing American Character*. New York: Doubleday Anchor Books.

Róheim, Géza. 1968. *The Origin and Function of Culture*. New York: Nervous and Mental Disease Monographs.

Rowling, J. K. 1998. *Harry Potter and the Sorcerer's Stone*. New York City, New York: Scholastic.

———. 1999. *Harry Potter and the Chamber of Secrets*. New York: Scholastic.

———. 1999. *Harry Potter and the Prisoner of Azkaban*. New York: Scholastic.

———. 2007. *Harry Potter and the Deathly Hallows*. New York: Arthur A. Levine Books.

Salinger, J. D. 1991. *The Catcher in the Rye*. New York: Little Brown.

Sarno, John E., MD. 1998. *The Mindbody Prescription: Healing the Body, Healing the Pain*. New York: Warner Books.

Sebold, Alice. 2002. *Lucky: A Memoir*. New York: Picador.

Shakespeare, William. 1971. *Romeo and Juliet*. New York: Washington Square Press.

Steinbeck, John. 1978. *Of Mice and Men*. New York: Penguin.

———. 2002. *East of Eden*. New York: Penguin.

———. 2006. *In Dubious Battle*. New York: Penguin.

Stevenson, Robert Louis. 1984. *Dr. Jekyll and Mr. Hyde*. New York: Random House.

Storr, Anthony. 1970. *Human Aggression*. New York: Bantam.

Sullivan, Harry Stack. 1997. *The Interpersonal Theory of Psychiatry*. New York: W. W. Norton.

Sun Tzu. 1971. *The Art of War*. Translated by Samuel B. Griffith. Oxford, UK: Oxford University Press.

Suzuki, D. T. 1974. *An Introduction to Zen Buddhism*. New York: Causeway Books.

Twain, Mark. 1981. *The Adventures of Huckleberry Finn*. New York: Bantam.

———. 2004. *The Adventures of Tom Sawyer*. New York: Bantam Dell.

Walls, Jeannette. 2009. *The Glass Castle: A Memoir*. New York: Scribner.

Watts, Alan. 1989. *The Way of Zen*. New York: Vintage Press.

Wickes, Frances G. 1978. *The Inner World of Childhood*. Boston, Massachusetts: Sigo Press.

Wright, Richard. 1993a. *Black Boy*. New York: HarperCollins.

Wright, Richard. 1993b. *Native Son*. New York: HarperCollins.

Audio-visual and online

Dretzin, Rachel (producer and director) and Douglas Rushkoff (correspondent). *Digital Nation*. Frontline program, aired February 2, 2010. http://www.pbs.org/wgbh/pages/frontline/digitalnation/.

Free, William (producer). 1996. "Mythos I: The Shaping of Our Mythic Tradition." Joseph Campbell Foundation. DVD (280 minutes).

Goodman, Barak (director). 2001. *The Merchants of Cool*. Frontline program, aired February 27, 2001. http://www.pbs.org/wgbh/pages/frontline/shows/cool/etc/credits.html.

Patillo, David, and Dorene Manchi (producers). 1988. "Joseph Campbell and the Power of Myth with Bill Moyers." Del Mar, California. Apostrophe S. Productions, in association with Alvin H. Perlmuttter, Inc. and Public Affairs Television, Inc. DVD (360 minutes).

Walker, Casey. 1998. "Waking Up to the Holographic Heart: Starting Over with Education." (Joseph Chilton Pearce, 1998 interview.) Reprinted from The Corporatization of Education edition of *Wild Duck Review* IV (2). http://www.ratical.org/many_worlds/JCP98.html.

Wallace, Mike (interviewer), and Erich Fromm. 1958. "The Mike Wallace Interview: Erich Fromm" (1958-05-25). http://www.youtube.com/watch?v=OTu0qJG0NfU&feature=results_video&playnext=1&list=PLE96DF861C7377461.

Index